OR · PLAN ·

16" = 1:0"
ELEVATION

SCALE · FOR · PLAN † ELEVATION ·

EVATION ·

E · HOUSE ·

MARYLAND ·

NOTE:
FOLLOWING · ISSUE · OF ·
THE · MONOGRAPH · SERIES ·
WILL · CONTAIN · MEASURED
DRAWINGS · OF · THE · INTERIOR
OF · THE · BRICE · HOUSE ·

MEAS † DRAWN · KENNETH CLARK ·

· SECTION ·

STYLES OF THE EMERGING NATION

Other National Historical Society Publications:

THE IMAGE OF WAR: 1861–1865

TOUCHED BY FIRE: A PHOTOGRAPHIC PORTRAIT OF THE CIVIL WAR

WAR OF THE REBELLION: OFFICIAL RECORDS
OF THE UNION AND CONFEDERATE ARMIES

OFFICIAL RECORDS OF THE UNION AND CONFEDERATE NAVIES
IN THE WAR OF THE REBELLION

HISTORICAL TIMES ILLUSTRATED ENCYCLOPEDIA OF THE CIVIL WAR

A TRAVELLER'S GUIDE TO GREAT BRITAIN SERIES

For information about National Historical Society Publications, write:
Historical Times, Inc., 2245 Kohn Road, Box 8200, Harrisburg, Pennsylvania 17105

Architectural Treasures of Early America

STYLES OF THE EMERGING NATION

From material originally published as
The Georgian Period
edited by
Professor William Rotch Ware

Lisa C. Mullins, Editor

Roy Underhill, Consultant

A Publication of
THE NATIONAL HISTORICAL SOCIETY

Library of Congress Cataloging-in-Publication Data

Styles of the emerging nation/Lisa C. Mullins, editor; Roy Underhill, consultant.
    (Architectural treasures of Early America; 13)
    1. Architecture, Georgian — New York (State).   2. Architecture, Colonial — New York (State).   3. Architecture — New York (State).
4. Architecture, Georgian — Pennsylvania — Philadelphia.
5. Architecture, Colonial — Pennsylvania — Philadelphia.
6. Architecture — Pennsylvania — Philadelphia.   7. Philadelphia, (Pa.) — — Buildings, structures, etc.   I. Mullins, Lisa C.   II. Series: Architectural Treasures of Early America (Harrisburg, Pa.); 13.
NA730.N4S88   1988   720'.9747 — dc19   88-1677
ISBN 0-918678-35-8

CONTENTS

THE TROUBLE WITH TIMBER

Imagine living in a house made of sugar, surrounded by billions of tiny, hungry Hansels and Gretels. That's the way it is with old wooden houses. Wood is a remarkably durable material composed of long chain molecules of simple sugars. It will not deteriorate on its own, but has to be attacked by decay fungi or wood-eating insects. They break the long sugar chains into small pieces and, left to themselves, can eat your house down. When you live in a wooden house, this little worry comes with the territory.

Why does some wood rot and other wood does not? Some trees put more poison in their hearts than others. Over the years, a tree dumps its waste products in the old dead inner wood. These natural poisons make the heartwood of many species decay resistant. Old growth heart pine or red cedar can resist anything except fire. The huge old trees of the early American forest built up a lot of this heartwood, and the houses built from this wood should still stand firm for centuries to come.

Some wood may decay sooner than others, but no wood will decay unless it stays damp. That's all it takes, because the spores of decay fungi are everywhere. Wherever a roof leaks, a crawl space is unventilated, or an end grain is exposed, there you may find decay. Bad paint can be worse than bare wood. When paint begins to break down, it lets water into the wood but will not allow it to get out.

What can you do if you discover signs of decay? Knocking the mushrooms off the wood does no more to kill the fungus than knocking the seed head off a dandelion. The essential step is to dry the wood out. Dry wood will not rot. If you dry the wood long enough the fungi will become dormant and eventually die. If the damage is severe, of course, or if moisture can not be controlled, the wood must be replaced by resistant or treated material. But try to control the moisture first, then resort to poisoned material. Ninety percent of wood problems are related to moisture.

Decay is the biggest problem with wood, but insects follow close behind. Many insects, like carpenter ants, just use the wood for shelter, others, like termites, use it for food, but both damage it by riddling it with tunnels.

Termites are the most feared of the wood eaters. But should you discover them, don't panic, you get into more trouble when you overreact. Even a large colony of termites can eat no more than half a pencil's worth of wood a day. Over the years this can add up to considerable sum, but contracts signed in panic and inept remedies can cause much more damage and expense. Annual inspection is your best defense. Look for earth tubes, piles of chaff, or discarded wings. Metal termite shields on top of the foundations are not positive protection, but they do force the termites to build their earth tubes out where you can see them. Tapping around suspect timbers with a hammer or probing with a screwdriver can reveal hidden damage. One company uses a trained dog that can sniff out infestations, but you can develop quite a knack for spotting the little devils on your own.

Damage from beetles is easier to detect because of the exit holes left on the surface of the wood. Tiny holes in timber are often made by beetles that attacked the wood while it was still green. They can't reinfest the dry wood in your home. The larvae of the powderpost beetles, lyctids, anobids, and bostrichid beetles, do attack timber in place, but pose less of a problem in occupied, centrally heated buildings. Beetle attacks can be halted by fumigating the building with poison gas, but this is a dangerous, expensive proposition and leaves no residual protection against another attack. If you think you have a problem, remember that expert help is available from your county extension agent or the local university. And don't panic.

A bigger beetle is the old house borer. The old house borer larvae lives for about seven years, eating its way up and down the length of a timber. When it matures, it bores its way out to mate, leaving a quarter inch diameter exit hole. The borer lays eggs and can reinfest the same area for decades. You can find out if the beetles are active by marking the existing exit holes and checking back every year for new ones. (Old house borers are shy creatures, though, and will usually abandon a house occupied by normal human teenagers.)

Some people with acute hearing can be driven to desperate measures by the old house borer. One couple moved into an old house that was shared by a family of old house borers. The husband worried through the night at their faint scratchings. Unable to stand it any longer, he bought a stethoscope and a long thin drill bit. In the silence of the night he listened for the sound of their chewing. Fearing to make any noise, he crept from the bed where his wife still slept. Gently he placed the stethoscope against the timber until he pinpointed the nocturnal gnawer. Quietly he took the cordless drill from the bedside table. Taking careful, breathless aim, he pulled the trigger on the drill, and with cries of "Die worm!" he riddled the spot on the timber with holes. Within a week, the last of the old house borers were gone—and so was his wife.

ROY UNDERHILL
MASTER HOUSEWRIGHT
COLONIAL WILLIAMSBURG

Colonial Architecture of the United States

Text by
Olof Z. Cervin
Originally published in 1898 as
Volume I of The Georgian Period

Detail of Doorway
211 SOUTH SEVENTEENTH STREET,
PHILADELPHIA, PENNSYLVANIA
A copy from an original on Front Street

THE SO-CALLED COLONIAL ARCHITECTURE OF THE UNITED STATES[1]

"Men can with difficulty originate, even in a new hemisphere." — EDWARD EGGLESTON

IT is proposed in this paper to gather together some of the records bearing upon the architecture of the seventeenth and eighteenth centuries, and to arrange these so as to furnish a short, systematic and comprehensive survey of what building activity was exercised within the English provinces of America during that time.

The art of this period — including also the first twenty years of the nineteenth century — is generally called Colonial. Some object to the term, saying that there is too much variety of style to come under one head, and that, moreover, the best work was executed long after the original colonies had become provinces, and even later. But the term has been in use so long, and is so suggestive and comprehensive, that it would be difficult to find one more acceptable. Object as we may to the words "Gothic" and "Colonial," we cannot spare them, for no other words call up in the mind so complete a picture, not only of architecture and of the other arts, but of all the peculiar conditions — social, religious and political — which produced the mediaeval ecclesiastical architecture of Europe and the eighteenth-century domestic architecture of America.

In this domestic architecture, there was evolution and growth, just as truly as in any other style. If the perfection of Greek art remained unaccountable until the archaeological discoveries on the banks of the Nile and the Euphrates, still less would one understand Colonial art without a knowledge of the preceding styles. America owes Europe much, and we shall see that the emigrants left the mother country with neither empty hands nor empty heads.

THE NEW ENGLAND PROVINCES: DOMESTIC ARCHITECTURE

The reason for beginning with the New England colonies is not because they are the oldest and furnish a good geographical starting point, but because in them is more and better material, more thoroughly investigated and recorded. Moreover, the architecture in them, being homogeneous, is more easily classified. By making a classification, the subsequent inquiry farther south will be made easier, for thus a standard or criterion will have been established to which references can be made.

After the first quarter of the eighteenth century there came to the colonist a period of comparative peace and prosperity. The Indian was no longer a standing menace, "the stubborn phalanx of forest trees had been gradually beaten back, the disencumbered fields yielded a surplus, and leisure and comfort compensated for hard beginnings." It is only natural to find architecture influenced by this. Almost all good Colonial work is later than 1730.

A brief review of the earlier period possesses, however, both interest and value. The subject can best be discussed under three topics: log houses, military homes and settlers' cottages.

The log house, the first and most natural dwelling[2] in a new and thickly wooded country, was not to the taste of the colonist. Life in it was to him a chrysalid state, from which to emerge, the sooner the better.

---

[1] Post-graduate thesis of Mr. Olof Z. Cervin, Architectural Department, School of Mines, Columbia College, 1894, revised and amplified.

[2] Mr. C. W. Ernst has recently discovered satisfactory evidence that the very first work of the settlers was to set up sawmills, that they might get out the lumber in the sizes and shapes which they were wont to handle at home. — WARE

Fig. 1. OLD STONE HOUSE — 1639 — GUILFORD, CONNECTICUT

Roughly squared timbers seemed incompatible with his higher ideals.

Yet the first Doric artisan, when called upon by his fellows to rear a worthy abode for the ancient *xoanon*, did not find it so. Looking about for suggestions, he saw nothing but the low-roofed timber houses of Homer's heroes. But in them his artistic sense perceived great possibilities. In the rough timber ends he found splendid triglyphs; in the open spaces, sculptured metopes; in the ungainly trunnels, depending guttae; and in the overhanging rafters, richly raised mutules.

But the colonist, disdaining the material at hand, cast longing glances back to Europe, and, from his earliest efforts to his last, there was ever a conscious striving to reproduce in this new land his former home, grown doubly dear through long separation. Thus Lowell says of Cambridge, that it looked like an English village badly transplanted.

Many settlers had for a long time no choice but to live in log houses. This fact they concealed as best they could be covering them with clapboards or shingles, put on with hand-wrought nails. The floor, often at first of stamped clay, was soon superseded by a pavement of rough puncheons. The window lights were of mica, of oiled paper, or of horn. No glass found its way to the colonies before the year 1700, or thereabouts.

The military homes were more important structures. As in the early settlements the prime requisite was protection against the elements, wild beasts and savage men, it was quite common that one or more of the houses should be built especially large and strong, to serve as a refuge and a rallying point, from which the more effectually to repel Indian onslaughts. Many stories and bloody legends still cling with the old moss and lichen to these silent witnesses of a danger-fraught period.

Important among those still standing are: the old brick house of Governor Cradock, built about 1634, at Medford, Massachusetts; the stuccoed timber house of Governor Bull, in Newport, Rhode Island, built in 1639; and the clapboarded Minot homestead, in Dorchester, Massachusetts, built in 1640. The so-called Old Stone House (Fig. 1), finished in 1640 as a parsonage, at Guilford, Connecticut, has since been rebuilt upon the original lines. The Red Horse Inn, at Sudbury, Massachusetts, built in 1680, and made famous through Longfellow's *Tales of a Wayside Inn,* though not known to have served as a fort, resembles the preceding so much as to readily group with them. The poet's words, descriptive of this inn, will be helpful in picturing this class of houses: —

> "As ancient is this hostelry
> As any in the land may be,
> Built in the old Colonial day,
> When men lived in a grander way,
> With ampler hospitality;
> A kind of old Hobgoblin Hall,
> Now somewhat fallen to decay,
> With weather stains upon the wall,
> And stairways worn, and craggy doors,
> And creaking and uneven floors,
> And chimneys huge and tiled and tall."

Architecturally, these structures are very simple. Leaving out the Old Stone House, which alone is irreg-

Fig. 2. CRADOCK HOUSE * — 1634 — MEDFORD, MASSACHUSETTS

This sketch, made in 1881, shows the house without the dormers here spoken of, which leaves it open to doubt whether these features may be recent additions.

* Speaking of the Cradock House, Prof. C. E. Norton writes: "It is more than a mere antiquarian or architectural curiosity. It illustrates more vividly than any other house in the neighborhood of Boston the condition and modes of life of the first generation of colonists."

Fig. 3. OLD MANSE, CONCORD,
MASSACHUSETTS

Fig. 5. JOHN QUINCY ADAMS'S HOUSE,
BOSTON, MASSACHUSETTS

ular and picturesque, the main elements are: a rectangular plan, two stories and an attic, a gambrel gable at each end, a symmetrical disposition of openings and dormers, and an overhang of the second, or of the attic story, for defense.

The Cradock House (Fig. 2), typical in its way, deserves special mention. It is the oldest house standing today in New England, and as that delightful chronicler, Drake, puts it, "proudly bears its credentials on its weather-beaten face." Though its English owner never saw it, his "servant" was conscientious in building it well. The design is thought to have been suggested by Cradock's London house. The timber was hewn within a few feet of the site, the bricks were burned on the spot. Iron guards were built into the doorways, and four dangerous looking loopholes showed that it was a military house first and a trading post and a home after. Two solid chimneys stand guard one at each end. Two dormers relieve the long roof expanse of the front. The original windows were small. There is no ornament except a plain band at the second-story level. In the main lines of its composition

it is strikingly like the Hancock House, of Boston, of which a *pseudo replica* was erected at the Columbian Exhibition, at Chicago. It would be interesting to know the arrangement of the rooms, but no plans are accessible. Even if the present partitioning off were known, it would be of little value, owing to probable interior remodeling. Undoubtedly, the planning was simple — a multitude of closets, odd corners, and easy staircases are modern conveniences, for even the later Colonial houses, though often elaborate and costly, were seldom comfortable, to our way of thinking.

Quite early another — a cottage — type was evolved, with a long sweeping roof towards the rear, canting off a corner of the ceiling of each story from the attic to the kitchen. This type persisted until quite recently and recurs in hundreds of cottages (Figs. 5, 6 and 7) throughout New England. Such were the childhood homes of the Presidents Adams (Fig. 5). It was just such an humble dwelling, in Easthampton, Long Island, whose fond memories re-echoed in the heart of John Howard Payne, and produced the song of "Home, Sweet Home."

Fig. 4. AVERY HOUSE, PEQUONNOCK,
CONNECTICUT

Fig. 6. OLD HOUSE — 1643 — PIGEON COVE,
MASSACHUSETTS

Fig. 7. BRADSTREET HOUSE, ANDOVER, MASSACHUSETTS

Fig. 9. OLD COTTAGE, PORTSMOUTH, NEW HAMPSHIRE

The doorway is the only "feature." There is usually on each side of the door a Classic pilaster, with a moulded capital, supporting a plain cornice with a pediment. Even this simple feature is often omitted.

To this period belong the historic Witch House, in Salem, and the home of Paul Revere, in Boston, neither of which groups readily with any of the above.

The peace and commercial prosperity, which set in about 1730, stimulated building activity. The shrewder merchants, having amassed considerable fortunes by traffic in slaves, lumber, fish, tea and English stuffs, set themselves to the pleasing task of spending their gains. What better could they do than to erect commodious houses? Some professional men and some landed proprietors, too, had become wealthy, and vied with these merchants in their building enterprises. The ordinary material was wood; that is, houses were constructed of an open framework of timber and covered with clapboards, or sometimes with shingles. Brick was rarely employed, except in the larger towns.

Many, especially the earlier houses, seem to have been suggested by Governor Cradock's military home,

or by others similar. By degrees the gambrel roof was eliminated. First, the hipped or the mansard roof came into vogue, from about 1760 to 1790. This was in turn superseded by the flat deck, towards the close of the century. Of course, examples of each overlap, the gambrel type being specially persistent; but the general tendency will be clearly shown, in an appended chronological table.

The gambrel roof is, no doubt, the result of an effort to secure additional height in the attic space. Though the oldest, it is the most graceful and pleasing, avoiding the box-like effect and hard lines of the other two. Of this type, the following are noteworthy: the Pepperell mansion, at Kittery, Maine, begun about 1720, and confiscated after the Revolution with its thirty miles of property; the Hancock mansion, at Boston, begun in 1737; the birthplace of General Putnam, at Danvers, Massachusetts, built partly in 1650 and partly in 1744; and the often illustrated "King" Hooper House, also at Danvers, which was, in many things, a copy in wood of the Hancock House. The Hancock House, now a memory only, though one of

Fig. 8. OLD HOUSE — c1700 — FARMINGTON, CONNECTICUT

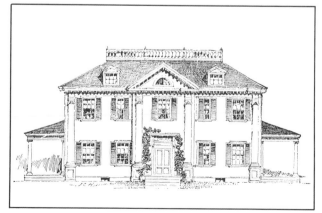

Fig. 10. VASSALL-CRAIGIE-LONGFELLOW HOUSE — 1759 — CAMBRIDGE, MASSACHUSETTS

the oldest, was one of the best. It was a stone building, so solidly erected as to require blasting when torn down. Thomas Hancock began it in 1737. Having become immensely wealthy, for those days, through skillful trading, he felt that Boston was getting too crowded for him. Just outside its limits he found a fine hill overlooking the bay. Here he staked out his house, fifty-six feet wide. When completed, he improved the grounds with walks and gardens. The entrance, in the middle of the front, was protected by a balcony, opening from the wide hallway of the second story. On the sides were two large windows in each story. Three dormers lighted the attic. A modillion cornice, returning on itself at the ends, marked the transition from the wall to the roof. A balustrade of neat spindles surrounded entirely the upper and flatter slope—a connecting chain from chimney to chimney, justified only by the happy way in which it crowned the whole. The corners and openings were trimmed with white stone quoins. The details were refined and the ornament sparing, but appropriate. Altogether, it was a roomy, well-designed and dignified house, exactly suited to be the mansion of the first gentleman of the Commonwealth, and through him and his illustrious nephew, John Hancock, to extend its stately hospitality to the greatest men of the day. It lacked many important features. Thus there were no spacious verandas, no two-storied pilasters, and no gable over the front entrance. The second, or mansard type, is more Classic, presenting on all sides a predominance of horizontal lines. But the elements of the design are virtually the same. The roof balustrade is usually, as it should be, placed around the flat deck on top. Sometimes it occurs at the base of the slope.

The Vassall mansion (Fig. 10), built in 1759, at Cambridge, Massachusetts, and since 1837 the home of Longfellow, is a splendid example of this class. The large Oliver House, at Dorchester, Massachusetts, built in 1740, the birthplace of Edward Everett, is also a worthy structure, in spite of its steep box-like roof and lack of verandas. The Quincy mansion, Quincy, Massachusetts, built in 1770, is quite remarkable with its attic rising like a clerestory above the outside walls. Many other prominent examples could be quoted.

The flat-roofed houses (Fig. 12), forming the third class, are less interesting. The details are stiff, and there is a tendency to formalism. Many of these are three stories in height. In Boston, they were often four stories high and of brick. There is in this type a certain meagerness. The porches are small and bare, the columns few and slender. Evidently, the original inspiration had begun to fail, and there was a striving for new effects.

The birthplace and home of Lowell, known as

Fig. 11. ELMWOOD, CAMBRIDGE, MASSACHUSETTS

Built early in the eighteenth century.

Elmwood, at Cambridge, is as fine and typical an example of this class as is Longfellow's of the preceding. Elmwood is three stories high, the upper story, however, more like a mezzanine (Fig. 11). It stands charmingly among high trees planted by the poet's father.

Naturally enough, few names of designers have been handed down. It is, therefore, a pleasure to record some. William Spratz, a Hessian soldier, was the architect of the Deming House, at Litchfield, Con-

Fig. 12. BRADLEE OR "BOSTON TEA-PARTY" HOUSE, 1771, AND HOLLIS STREET CHURCH, 1810
BOSTON, MASSACHUSETTS
The "Tea-Party House" was pulled down in 1898 and the Hollis Street Church, the tower removed, was in 1885 remodeled into a theatre.

necticut, built in 1790. It has a low mansard roof, with a balustrade just over the cornice. The middle portion slightly projecting and finished with a pediment, has, in the second story, a fine Palladian window, very similar to one found in a brick house at Annapolis, Maryland. (See Fig. 75.) The details are very correct and elegant, as though designed with *Vignola* in the hand. The general effect is pleasing, except that the cornice lacks a frieze, which gives it the appearance of having sunk into the wall.

The mere fact that Spratz was a soldier throws some light upon the status of the architectural profession. The provinces possessed, we might say, no educated architects. Most houses were the result of collaboration of owner and village carpenter. The one furnished the general plan and ideas, the other worked out the details. Thus Dr. Ayrault, in 1739, specified in his contract, still existing, that the builders were to provide a hood over the entrance, and to support the same on carved brackets (Fig. 13). Such notices, and some accidentally preserved books on the Orders, by Swan, Pain, Langley and others, indicate that the colonial mechanic was more than a mere skillful tool. He expended thought in devising practical methods for executing in wood Classic features and details originally designed for stone construction. Many characteristics, such as a tendency to increase the proportional height of the columns (Fig. 14), and details like the one illustrated in Figure 15, may be traced to these efforts.

FEATURES

A few words on each of the more important features will serve to give a clearer idea of what good Colonial residences really were: —

The entrance, which ought to be one of the principal external features, was never neglected by the colonial builders. A shell hood, carried on brackets, just over the pilaster-flanked door was a common and simple device (Fig. 13). The idea was directly borrowed from England, there adapted from the upper part of a niche.

More frequently the pilasters support a cornice and a pediment. In the best examples the details are carefully wrought, with carved Corinthian or Ionic capitals. The Ionic capitals usually have Composite scrolls, a variety often occurring in Colonial work. Sometimes the modillions, too, were carved, but more often they were left plain, as in Figure 20.

Another device was to leave the doorway itself very simple, and flank it with semidetached columns or pilasters rising through two stories, as in Longfellow's house (Fig. 10). Often, though not always, pilasters were placed on or near the house corners also. This

Fig. 13. *Hood*
AYRAULT HOUSE, NEWPORT, RHODE ISLAND

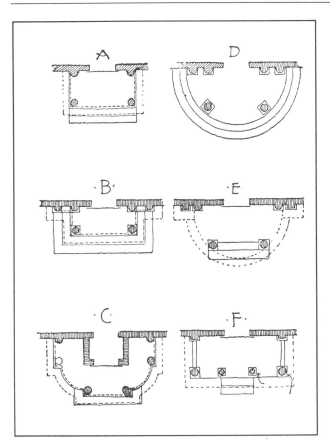

Fig. 14. A. PIERCE HOUSE, 1780, SALEM, MASSACHUSETTS

B. HURD HOUSE, 1795, CHARLESTOWN, MASSACHUSETTS

C. GOVERNOR LANGDON HOUSE, 1784, PORTSMOUTH, NEW HAMPSHIRE

D. MOUNT GRIDDELL HOUSE, 1800, CHARLESTOWN, MASSACHUSETTS

E. TUCKER HOUSE, 1808, SALEM, MASSACHUSETTS

F. COUNT RUMFORD'S HOUSE, WOBURN, MASSACHUSETTS

high order involved so wide a frieze in the entablature that it was either entirely omitted, or it occurred only over the columns or pilasters. In some rare instances the frieze is wide enough to permit of an additional low story on a level with it.

A step toward greater elaboration was to add columns in front of those against the wall, and thus to produce a small portico, usually of flight projection (Fig. 14 A, B). Old buildings in New Haven and in other Connecticut towns show an ingenious adaptation of Michaelangelo's device in the Farnese Palace, at Rome, where the frieze of the entablature over each window is cut into by the opening (Fig. 17). Many small porches by this means gain sufficient height for

the doorway without crowding the pediment above the second-story window sills—a clever solution of a frequently recurring problem. A variation was to omit the free columns and to let the porch extend as a hood over the entrance (Figs. 18, 19). These schemes, however, were not sufficiently elaborate for all owners, and many entrance porches were developed into elaborate verandas, the columns, in some cases, disposed with much ingenuity (Fig. 14 C, E).

The two-story veranda, with colossal columns, though not common, occurs in some instances. Count Rumford's house, at Woburn, Massachusetts, has such a porch, with the additional device of the second story carried on a smaller order, similar to the main order (Fig. 14 F). It need hardly be said that these colossal orders are a failure, for, if two-story pilasters against the wall dwarf the entire structure, free-standing columns, gaining prominence by projection, have the same effect to a greater degree.

Many Colonial verandas are of generous proportions, cool and inviting. Often, as in Longfellow's home, there are two, though not always, as in this case, balancing one another.[3]

Much attention was bestowed upon the doorways. It was usual to enclose the doors with a framing of glass—transoms and sidelights—of great variety in treatment though fundamentally the same in idea.

The main cornice is, in general, well proportioned to the building: smaller in the earlier examples, in which it serves merely as a transition to the roof, than in the later structure, where it is itself the crowning member. In section, it is commonly based upon the Corinthian, though the modillions are seldom carved. Under the brackets, there is, in the best examples, a row of dentils, giving life and variety to the whole. The omission of the frieze and the use of colossal orders have already been mentioned.

Roof balustrades are of two varieties. One consists of light turned, or carved, spindles, with larger ones on the corners and at intervals of fifteen or twenty of the smaller ones. Sometimes square pedestals take their places. The other variety consists of some pattern of open latticework, in panels between pedestals. Figure 21 illustrates both varieties.

The corners gain an appearance of strength by the use of pilasters or of quoins. In several instances, the imitation courses of quoins are continued across the whole façade, so as to simulate stone rustication. Old "King" Hooper was not above pretending to live in a stone house. This spirit of pretension was the logical result of the one which considered it unbecoming to

---

[3] The side verandas were not parts of the original house, but were added by Mr. Longfellow. — WARE

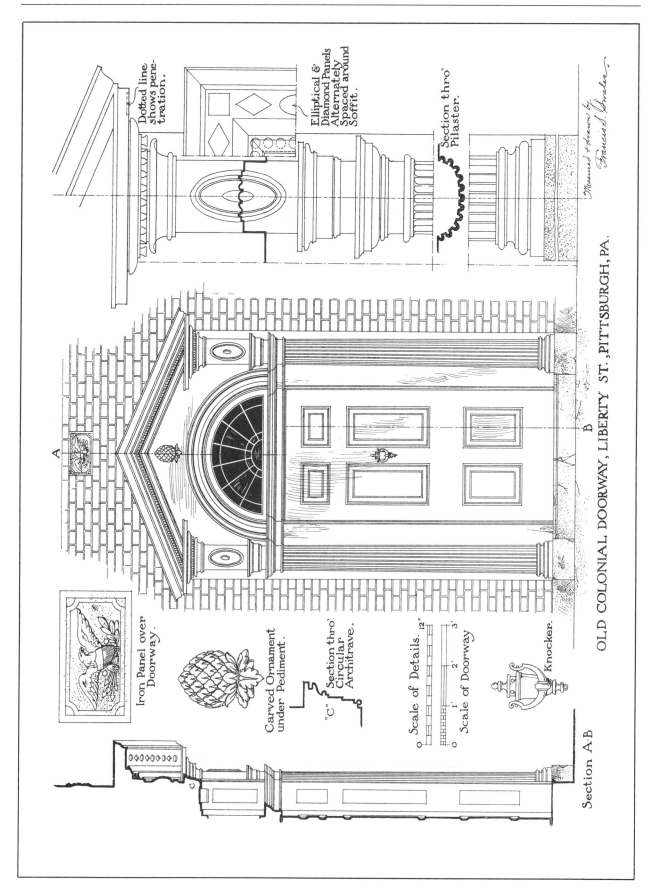

Dotted line shows penetration.

Elliptical & Diamond Panels Alternately Spaced around Soffit.

Section thro' Pilaster.

Measured & drawn by Francis S. Swales.

A

B

Iron Panel over Doorway.

Carved Ornament under Pediment.

"C" Section thro' Circular Architrave.

Scale of Details.

Scale of Doorway

Knocker.

Section A-B

OLD COLONIAL DOORWAY, LIBERTY ST., PITTSBURGH, PA.

St. Joseph's in the ·Courtyard· Willings Alley. Philada.

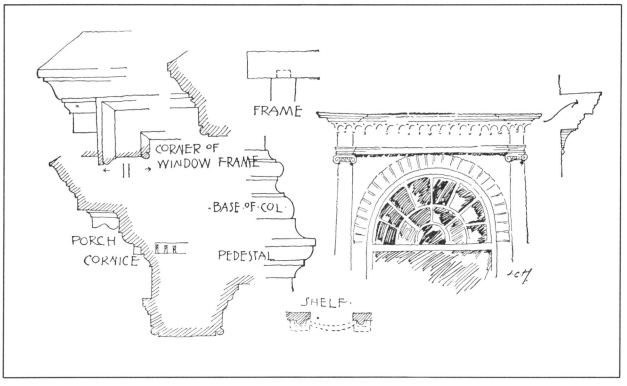

Fig. 15. *Window Finish, etc.*

Fig. 16. *Door Head* — PORTSMOUTH,
NEW HAMPSHIRE

Fig. 17. *Porch* — LITCHFIELD, CONNECTICUT

Fig. 18. *Porch*
TAYLOR HOUSE — 1790 — ROXBURY,
MASSACHUSETTS

Fig. 18a. TAYLOR HOUSE — 1790 —
ROXBURY, MASSACHUSETTS
Pulled down in 189-.

live in a log house, and so concealed the logs with clapboards or with shingles. But clapboards and shingles had better excuse, for they were useful in keeping out the cold.

A review of the exterior features would be incomplete without a reference to the so-called Palladian windows. A treatment of large openings, similar to that of Figure 75, from Maryland, occurred quite frequently in the New England and Middle colonies. Ultimately, the idea is derived from Palladio's ingenious device of two columns and two pilasters with an arch between the columns of a larger order. An interesting variety existed in the old Boston Library (Fig. 22).

Other windows are simply treated — often enclosed with some mouldings and a light cap over. An ingenious variation, from Massachusetts, is illustrated in Figure 15.

The treatment of dormers, too, is simple. Usually they are narrow and high, crowned with plain steep pediments, sometimes alternating with round or broken ones. Flat-roofed dormers were rare. The bold projections of the dormers from the roof constitute them one of the most striking features. It is strange that there was so little of effort for variety by giving the dormer greater breadth, and adding mullions, or even by developing it into a prominent gable. The gable (Fig. 23) from Count Rumford's house is quite unique.

Color is the only other exterior feature worthy of remark. Modern imitators would lead us to believe that it was universal to paint the ground a darker, usually a yellow, color, and pick out the trimmings in white. But few photographs show this — the color usually being a monotonous white. There are even some instances in which the trimmings are darker than the ground. An indefatigable inquirer tells us that originally Venetian red was universal. Yellow and white

came later. By carefully scraping off the successive coats of paint, red was found to underlie the others.

In brick buildings the trimmings were of white stone or quite often wood painted white, pleasingly contrasting with the general red tone.

INTERIORS

In the interior, the staircase hall, with its generous allotment of room, is quite remarkable. The hall can be made the most effective of all the rooms, for it has the first and the last chance to make a good impression upon the visitor. The value of this was not lost sight of, since Colonial houses seem to be the very embodiment of welcome and generosity.

The stairs are broad and the treads easy, with neat turned, or often hand-carved, scroll, balusters and newels. In some of the best examples carved brackets

Fig. 19. DOORWAY IN PROVIDENCE,
RHODE ISLAND

Fig. 20. *Porch*
HURD HOUSE — 1798 — CHARLESTOWN,
MASSACHUSETTS

Fig. 22. OLD LIBRARY, BOSTON,
MASSACHUSETTS
Charles Bulfinch, Architect

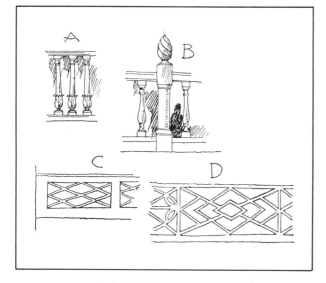

Fig. 21. A. FROM GOVERNOR LANGDON'S
HOUSE, 1784, PORTSMOUTH, NEW HAMPSHIRE
B. FROM KING HOOPER'S HOUSE, 1754,
   DANVERS, MASSACHUSETTS
C. FROM HALL HOUSE, 1785, MEDFORD,
   MASSACHUSETTS
D. FROM COUNT RUMFORD'S HOUSE,
   WOBURN, MASSACHUSETTS

Fig. 23. *Rear Dormer*
COUNT RUMFORD'S HOUSE, WOBURN,
MASSACHUSETTS

ornament and in detail. The orders often used to support the shelf are, with the greatest propriety, attenuated, sometimes to even twice the usual number of diameters, or even more. Much handcarving occurs, such as delicate fluting, balls, beads, eggs-and-darts, figures and geometric patterns, and a very charming, low-relief ornament, based upon the decorative work of the brothers Adam, in England (Figs. 26, 29). French rococo ornament is to be found in some very rare instances only.

It is worthy of notice, that though the Italian rococo spread to most countries and stamped its characteristics upon every branch of art, the New England colonies escaped almost unharmed. Rococo as a period of art was in them unknown. Some instances of rococo are found in the ceilings, the twisted balusters, and in some broken pediments. The Colonial style, though adapted from Classic motives, never became very formal, and so never felt the need of a reaction. This style did not succumb through the throwing off of all restraint, but through the Greek Revival and through the almost simultaneous second flood of immigration in the beginning of this century.

The treatment of the door and window finish exhibits almost every variety which the Renaissance has

Fig. 24. *Detail of Newel*
GOVERNOR LANGDON HOUSE, PORTSMOUTH,
NEW HAMPSHIRE

decorated each tread, similar to that shown by Figure 80, from the South. The modern idea of having one or two intermediate landings was rarely used.

The ceilings often have a richly moulded cornice with Corinthian modillions. The flat surface is sometimes decorated with some pattern ornament in plaster (Fig. 29), though it was more often left plain. A similar treatment is sometimes applied to the soffit of the stairs.

The walls were wainscoted, after the English manner, usually three feet high or so, though often all the way up to the ceiling, in large panels of wood. In some of the best houses Dutch scenic wall paper was preferred.

The fireplaces, with their mantelpieces often carried up to the ceiling, are the main features of the other rooms. These mantels are remarkable for delicacy in

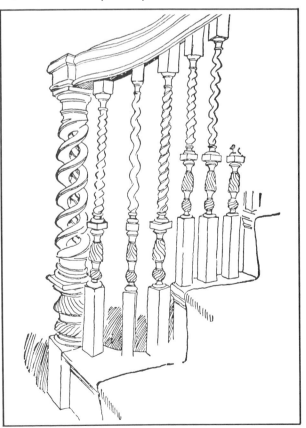

Fig. 25. *Detail of Stair*
HODGE'S HOUSE, SALEM, MASSACHUSETTS

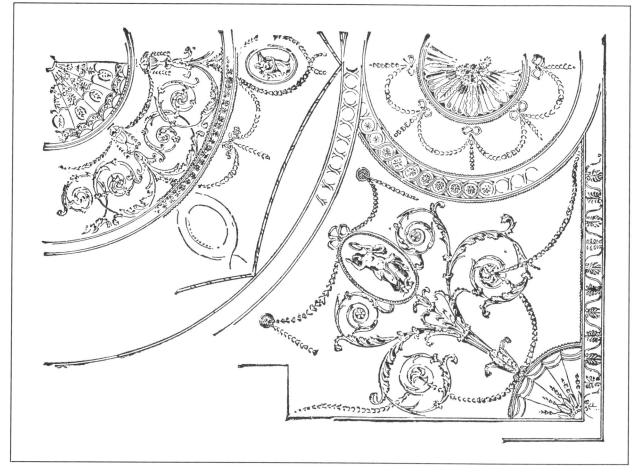

Fig. 26. PORTION OF AN "ADAMS" CEILING.
PERIOD FROM 1760.

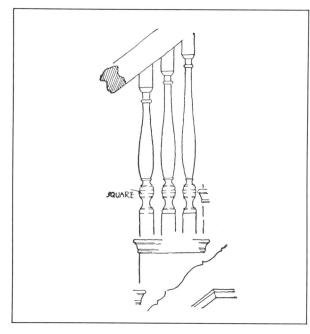

Fig. 27. *Stair*—LITCHFIELD, CONNECTICUT

Fig. 28. *Corner Cupboard*—JAFFREY HOUSE,
PORTSMOUTH, NEW HAMPSHIRE

Fig. 29. *Plaster Ceiling*—SALEM, MASSACHUSETTS

which, with their prim gables, seem magically transported from England. Another source of picturesqueness is that of gradual addition to a small nucleus, as in Figure 4. Peter Avery had bought a condemned church and this he tried to incorporate with the older part of his home. The result is certainly quaint.

We have in the preceding considered a series of homes of the people, structures far less pretentious than, and, therefore, not comparable with, the palaces of Italy, the châteaux of France, or the manors of England. Although every detail of our Colonial work might be traced to some European prototype, the general resemblance is slight. Time, distance and materials contributed on this side of the water to produce a style of domestic architecture of marked individuality, dignified without being formal, pure, simple, home-like and peerless. Peerless—yes; for, whether it be that this is the only domestic architecture worthy of much consideration, or that only Americans have thought it worth while to study the houses of their forefathers, it is a fact that no other style is nearly so fully recorded, or illustrated in so abundant a literature.

Fig. 30. *Doorway*—SALEM, MASSACHUSETTS

bequeathed to us. Flanking pilasters with plain, broken or carved pediments occur frequently. If any one thing can be said to be characteristic, it is the decoration of the panels, either carved or of putty, with motives just spoken of as borrowed from the brothers Adam (Figs. 30, 31). Ultimately, they are based upon Roman festoons. The modeling is so exquisite, and they are, moreover, capable of so much variety in disposition as to justify the eagerness with which the colonists used them. Happy, indeed, is the evolution of the heavy Roman festoon to a string of forget-me-nots, each smaller than the preceding, each festoon bound to the next with a delicate ribbon. The door finish designs (Figs. 30, 31) are well worthy of emulation.

Of necessity, all the peculiarities have not been pointed out, nor, indeed, have all types been referred to. The reader's mind has perhaps reverted to tales of romance which have endued colonial life with absorbing interest. *The House of Seven Gables* (Fig. 32) may, in advance, have suggested a complete picture; a picture full of turrets and gables and all manner of broken skylines, but nothing of simple, dignified, Classical fronts. But Hawthorne, according to his son's biography, had little sense of locality or taste for absolutely correct description. Though he did not invent his architecture, he did that which is hardly less deceptive: he picked out exceptional cases and altered these to suit his fancy, which found but little of value in Classic symmetry.

Picturesqueness, though not a charateristic, is not entirely lacking. It occurs mostly in cottages, some of

Fig. 31. *Parlor Door*
NICHOLSON-PIERCE HOUSE—1780—
SALEM, MASSACHUSETTS

Fig. 32. HOUSE OF THE SEVEN
GABLES—1668—SALEM, MASSACHUSETTS

PUBLIC ARCHITECTURE: CHURCHES

But there was other building than that of dwellings. Some public structures still remain, and many have been demolished to be replaced by later buildings. It is a pleasure to note that the general sentiment is now strong for preserving the few old-time mementos we still have. Several have been restored. These are, however, rarely of much intrinsic value, possessing, as they do, little of originality, and being generally poor copies of transatlantic works.

After considerable searching, I have found but scanty material. Fifteen churches and eight secular buildings constitute my entire list for New England. It is possible that there was but little use for town houses and city halls: the "meeting houses," serving also other than devotional purposes, helped to supply their places.

The earliest of these "meeting houses" were plain and bare to the point of rudeness. Puritan sentiment did not countenance display or even limited decora-

tion, and discarded the very word "church," because associated with so much outward show.

The usual type, according to Dr. Eggleston, was square in plan. On the exterior were two stories of windows. The steep roof, sloping from the four sides, was surmounted by a belfry with a slender spire, the bell-rope dangling in the middle of the assembly room. Such was the famous "Old Ship" at Hingham, Massachusetts. This type was much more suited for a schoolhouse than for a place of worship, though not *per se* devoid of artistic possibilities.

Some were of still ruder forms, often mere barns. Occasionally a small hexagonal plan was adopted (Fig. 33). One would be glad to find in poverty and in the date of their erection an excuse for such inappropriate forms and crude ideas—but many contemporary residences still exist to testify to much taste combined with great simplicity. Moreover, small and artistic churches are found farther south. Poverty is no excuse for poor design.

An old church at Narraganset, Rhode Island, is

A CHRONOLOGICAL TABLE OF SOME IMPORTANT NEW ENGLAND "COLONIAL" RESIDENCES.

Building	Date	Location	Authority	Roof
Cradock House	1634	Medford, Mass.	Drake	Gambrel ...
Standish "	1636	Duxbury, "	Century	" ...
Bull "	1639	Newport, R.I.	Am. Arch. ..	" ...
Minot Homestead	1640	Dorchester, Mass.	Drake	Gable .....
The Red Horse Inn	1680	Sudbury, "	"	Gambrel ...
Old Indian House	1680	Deerfield, "	"	Gable .....
Grant "	about 1770	Newport, R.I.	Am. Arch. ..	Gambrel ...
Warner "	1723	Portsmouth, N.H.	Photo	" ...
Pepperell "	1725	Kittery, Me.	Drake	" ...
Thompson "	1730	Woburn, Mass.	Am. Arch. ..	" ...
Walker "	1734	Concord, "	" " ...	" ...
Hancock "	1737	Boston, "	Drake	" ...
Hobgoblin Hall	1740	Medford, "	"	" ...
Dalton House........	1740	Dorchester, "	"	Mansard ...
Everett "	1740	Newburyport, "	Photo	Gambrel ...
Putnam "	1744	Danvers, "	Drake	" ...
Adams "	1750	Quincy, "	"	" ...
Wells Place	1752	Weathersfield, Conn. ...	Am. Arch. ..	" ...
Hooper House	1754	Danvers, Mass.	Drake	" ...
Vassall "	1759	Cambridge, "	Photo	Mansard ...
Derby "	1760	Salem, "	"	Gambrel ...
Bannister " ......)	between	Newport, R.I.	Am. Arch. ..	" ...
Vernon " ......{	1750	" "	" " ..	Mansard ...
Gibbs " ......{	and	" "	" " ..	" ...
Hazard " ......)	1776	" "	" " ..	Flat ....
Quincy "	1770	Quincy, Mass.	Drake	" ...
Pierce "	1780	Salem, "	Photo	" ...
"Elmwood"	about 1780	Cambridge, "	"	" ...
Babson House	1781	Newburyport, "	"	" ...
Langdon "	1784	Portsmouth, N.H.	"	Mansard ...
Hall "	1785	Medford, Mass.	"	Gambrel ...
Hall "	1789	" "	"	Mansard ...
Taylor "	1790	Weymouth, "	"	Flat ....
Arnold "	1790	Boston, "	"	Mansard ...
Hurd "	1795	Charlestown, "	"	Flat ....
Appleton "	about 1800	Boston, "	"	" ...
Carrington "	" 1800	Providence, R.I.	"	" ...
Baldwin "	" 1800	Salem, Mass.	"	" ...
Hodge "	" 1800	" "	"	" ...
Otis "	" 1800	Boston, "	"	" ...

Fig. 33. FRIENDS' MEETING HOUSE,
BURLINGTON, NEW JERSEY

slightly better. In it the lower, and taller, story of windows has round heads, and the doorway, too, is something more than a mere opening with a hinged flap.

It was impossible for the ultra-Puritan asceticism to continue indefinitely. A reaction must set in, and man's inborn love for beauty must find some expression. The evil seed, however, had been sown, and there are those who attribute the decadence of the church in New England, partially at least, to this long refusal to satisfy aesthetic requirements.

Christ Church at Shrewsbury, New Jersey, an improvement upon the Narraganset church, is doubly interesting. It is a church unmistakably, and of a type which has later been copied in hundreds of our western towns—an oblong plan with four to six round-headed windows on each side, a pediment with a bull's-eye window at each end, and a belfry bursting through the roof in front. The two front doorways, where one would be sufficient, have an interest, recalling, as they do, the social custom of featuring the men and women on different sides of the church, with a barrier throughout the length to separate the young folks. This church is frame and shingled; many like it are clapboarded. The details are Classic, rather freely treated. This kind of a church is at most suited for the country or for a village. In a growing town it is soon brushed aside and replaced by another.

These superseding churches form a class by themselves. More citified and substantial, they are usually of brick or of stone. Their design is so directly based

Fig. 34. PARK STREET STEEPLE, BOSTON,
MASSACHUSETTS

CANVAS

SEAT

Fig. 35. *Pulpit*
KING'S CHAPEL, BOSTON, MASSACHUSETTS

upon the Wren churches of London as to deceive any except close scrutiny. The towers are, perhaps, more tapering and graceful, and the churches throughout seem to be better built. These towers—in composition Gothic, in details Renaissance—are the prominent features. The scheme is simple: a square base, several contracting, usually octagonal, stories, and a steep crowning spire. These tower stories are treated with the orders, cornices, pediments, balustrades and large scrolls, used with much variety, though often rather awkwardly, for few elements could be less tractable in spire composition. Such towers are found all the way from New England to the Carolinas. The Park Street Church, Boston, steeple, Peter Banner, architect, is one of the finest of this class.

The Old South Church, too, at Boston, is a well-known structure. In this the square part of the tower rises high above the main roof-ridge. The transition to the one-story octagon is concealed by a balustrade. The slender, soaring spire is fine indeed, with its four lofty dormers at the base.

The interiors, too, follow English models. Thus St. James's Church, Piccadilly, has in Christ Church, Boston, an echo of that peculiar ceiling treatment in which the barrel-vault of the main aisle is intersected by small transverse vaults over the bays of the side aisles. The heaviness of this arrangement is skillfully avoided in St. Martin's-in-the-Fields, by making the cross-vaults intersect longitudinal vaults over all three aisles. This is echoed in King's Chapel, Boston, the cradle of Unitarianism in the United States. The Chapel is even an improvement, for here the coupled columns justify the block of entablature over them in a manner single columns cannot do. This interior, in almost pure white, is said to be one of the finest remaining from those days.

Church furniture, especially the pulpits and founding-boards, show much thought and care. The fine pulpit of King's Chapel (Fig. 35), in use since 1686, is ascended over narrow steps inclosed by a balustrade of hand-carved, spiral spindles. The delicate mouldings of the pulpit and of the sounding-board are broken above and below the pilasters, which are set back a little from the corner, thus giving much light and shade. Trinity Church of Newport, Rhode Island, can also boast of a well-designed and similar pulpit. A crown, the last of royal insignia in the states, is still poised on Trinity's lofty spire.

SECULAR BUILDINGS

The few remaining secular buildings show simplicity of taste and propriety in design. Three out of the eight buildings above referred to belong to Newport, and

PARK STREET CHURCH — 1809 —
BOSTON, MASSACHUSETTS

PARK STREET CHURCH — 1809 —
BOSTON, MASSACHUSETTS

Fig. 36. FIRST UNITARIAN CHURCH—1784—ELIOT SQUARE, ROXBURY, BOSTON, MASSACHUSETTS

their recording is due to the patriotism of George C. Mason, an architect of that city.[4]

These buildings illustrate two state houses and a library[5] at Boston, a library and a town house at Newport, a town house at Weathersfield, Connecticut, a market at Newport, and a customhouse at Salem. If to these we add a synagogue at Newport, my entire list is exhausted. All of these buildings date from 1740 to 1800.

It is difficult to classify so few buildings, and it would be hazardous to generalize, for to do that would be to assume that these examples are typical, whereas they may be, as is the Old State House (Fig. 39), at Boston, quite unique.

We have already seen that the best churches were based upon English models. That many of the civic buildings, also, had English elements may be inferred from the fact that Peter Harrison, the architect of the market at Newport (Fig. 38), and of other buildings there and elsewhere, had been an assistant to the famous Sir John Vanbrugh.

The name of another early Newport architect is also recorded: Richard Munday started in active life as a partner in the building business with Benjamin Wyatt. But Munday was made of ambitious stuff and ere long offered his services as an independent designer. He must have been successful, for in 1738 the town of Newport saw fit to entrust him with the design and erection of its new town house (Fig. 40). This building is symmetrical, well-proportioned and quiet, but it lacks the architectural character of Harrison's somewhat later works. For suggestion, Munday depended upon the type then in vogue for larger residences, previously described. He increased the dimensions, added another window on each side of the door, placed an octagonal cupola on the roof, and gave dignity to the whole by raising it upon a rustic basement five feet high. The dimensions are forty feet by eighty. Honestly constructed of brick and stone, it bravely promises to weather the seasons for many generations yet to come.

The old library at Boston (Fig. 22) and the market at Newport (Fig. 38) are both in the Palladian style, somewhat after the manner of the brothers Adam, England.

Boston is fortunate in still retaining two fine state houses. The older, more picturesque and interesting, covering a small plot of ground with streets close upon all sides, shows, strangely enough, decided Dutch in-

[4] The omission from this short list of Fanueil Hall by Peter Smibert and, later, Charles Bulfinch must be quite accidental. — WARE
[5] The building here mentioned was destroyed many years before this paper was written. — WARE

fluences in its singly-stepped end-gables with *affronté* lion and unicorn, and in its S-shaped exterior wall-anchors. The new State House, on the other hand, is a model of Classicality. Its prominent features are several flights of broad steps up the hill, a projecting arcade of the first story, with an open colonnade of single and coupled columns above, and a high, domineering gilded dome. The building is only two stories high, on a low basement. It was built in 1795 and was one of the most important undertakings of its time. Charles Bulfinch, its architect, was born in Boston, 1763. He spent some time in Europe after graduating. The successful feature of this design is the colonnade surmounting the arcade, with the unusual disposition of two pairs of columns at each end and four single in between. The dome, too, is fine. But it is hard not to believe it to be elastic or springy, partaking something of the nature of a balloon.

The customhouse at Salem (Fig. 41) is very pleasing and appropriate. This building gains additional interest from association with Hawthorne. Here it was that he first conceived the romance of the *Scarlet Letter*.

The meagerness of this part of the review is all the more deplorable, for public buildings should be, and in most countries are, the outcome of a community's best efforts. But this very poverty of structure illustrates better than anything else could that our Colonial architecture was mainly a domestic architecture.

THE MIDDLE PROVINCES: DOMESTIC ARCHITECTURE

When Nieuw Amsterdam became New York, only about sixty years after is founding, the Dutch had already impressed many of their characteristics upon its architecture. Of these, some were soon outgrown, others persisted for a long time. It is quite natural that English elements at last prevailed. But there is, after all, only a slight resemblance between the architecture of New England and that of the Middle states. In some localities English influence hardly has been felt at all.

In New York City but little of the old work remains. One might expect that this city, with its 24,000 inhabitants in 1776, would have left us important structures. But fires and progress have made great havoc, or, as Richard Grant White cleverly phrases it: "Old New York has been swept out of existence by the great tidal wave of its own material prosperity." But what remains is always interesting and valuable, often priceless.

The entire field is the one least investigated by writers upon architecture. An attempt to classify the few examples of which data are obtainable might prove futile. It is, however, certainly interesting to note pe-

Fig. 37. *Spire*
CONGREGATIONAL CHURCH,
MANCHESTER-BY-THE-SEA, MASSACHUSETTS

Fig. 38. MARKET OR CITY
HALL—1760—NEWPORT, RHODE ISLAND
Peter Harrison, Architect

Fig. 39. THE OLD STATE HOUSE, BOSTON,
MASSACHUSETTS

Fig. 40. TOWN HOUSE, LATELY STATE
HOUSE—1743—NEWPORT, RHODE ISLAND
Richard Munday, Architect

Fig. 41. THE CUSTOMHOUSE, SALEM,
MASSACHUSETTS

Fig. 42. DUTCH MANOR, LONG ISLAND,
NEW YORK

Fig. 44. ELSIE GERRETSEN
HOUSE—1781—FLATBUSH AVENUE,
BROOKLYN, NEW YORK

culiarities and points of similarity or dissimilarity between the Colonial work of this and of other sections.

New York was not only the most tolerant of all the colonies towards religious beliefs, but it was also the most eclectic and cosmopolitan in all matters, including building. Even before the peaceful English occupation eighteen languages were spoken in the city of New York, then having only 1,500 inhabitants. This little Babel welcomed every style of architecture and every kind of building material. In New England we found wood to be a characteristic. In the Southern colonies frame structures were, as we shall see, extremely rare. But in the Middle colonies, as was eminently proper, wood and stone, brick and stucco were employed. The roofs were covered with every available material—slate, shingles or tile, tin, lead or copper.

It has been pointed out how despised the log cabin was in New England. It was, if possible, still less thought of in this section. No Dutchman is known ever to have erected one for his dwelling. If he ever was forced to such a dire necessity, he must have succeeded, sooner than did his northern fellow colonist, in replacing it with something more acceptable.

Nor did the typical New England cottage, with its long sweep of roof, find much favor. Some do occur, but the Dutchman preferred to have a long slope to the front as well as the rear (Figs. 42, 45 and the Verplanck House).

Splendid Classical fronts, such as that of Longfellow's home, are rare indeed. The few that belong to this type generally lack any attempt at strict correctness in detail and monumentality in treatment.

Much, too, is lost by the absence of roof balustrades. For, though these are certainly without any practical value on a pitched roof, they seem almost indispensable for a good finish, at least for large

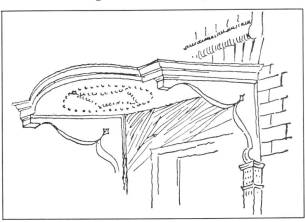

Fig. 43. *Door Hood*
VAN RENSSELAER HOUSE, GREENBUSH,
NEW YORK

Fig. 45. LEFFERTS FAMILY HOMESTEAD,
563 FLATBUSH AVENUE, BROOKLYN,
NEW YORK

Fig. 46. TYPICAL NEW YORK DORMER

Fig. 48. *Door* – FROM THE HOUSE OF NEW YORK'S THIRD MAYOR

Fig. 47. *Dormers* – NEWCASTLE, ENGLAND

Fig. 49. OLD DOORWAY, 116TH STREET, NEW YORK CITY

Fig. 50. VAN RENSSELAER MANOR HOUSE, GREENBUSH, NEW YORK

houses. But there were few lofty houses. The phlegmatic Hollander looked upon long flights of stairs as a nuisance. His ceiling was high enough if it was eight or nine feet above the floor. There seemed to him to be no use for a second story, when an attic might do. His house tended rather to horizontal dimensions.

Very few absolutely new features are encountered. The stepped gable, which occurred only sporadically in New England, was here found at every turn, from the Hudson to the Susquehanna. Very old prints show rows of these gables facing the streets. By degrees they disappear, and even as early as the Revolution they were not very common.

The gambrel roof, which was not used very often, was much modified. Sometimes it included two stories of windows, as in Figure 42. The upper slope was reduced in size, so as to become, in many cases, quite insignificant. The long, lower slope was, as in very early New England examples, gracefully curved, so as to soften its angularity and hardness (Figs 42 and 45). Many of the ordinary gabled roofs, also, had a neat curve at the bottom of the slope, just at the overhang of the eaves. This overhang, too, is worthy of special notice. Farther north it occurred at every story-level, and gradually disappeared in later houses. But the Dutch retained it, though using it only at the eaves. Sometimes it was made so great as to become a stoop or porch, requiring supporting columns.[6] Hackensack, especially, has many such overhanging eaves.

The details, as before stated, are not very Classic, although generally derived from some Classic source. Many vagaries and oddities occur. It would be difficult to find a precedent for the hood over the rear door of

the "ancient" Van Rensselaer Manor, at Greenbush, New York (Fig. 43), or for the interior door-trim of a New York house (Fig. 48). Both are charming in their originality and independence.

Typical New York dormers (Fig. 46) are based, as the Connecticut porches previously described, upon Michaelangelo's window treatment. They continued to be built for a long time, and may still be found on many old houses of that city and its neighborhood. Another distinct type of dormer is in Figure 68. The accompanying sketch (Fig. 47) shows an English precedent from Newcastle.

Still another peculiarity was what might be termed "window tracery." In the large cities of Boston, New York and Philadelphia there was evolved a style of light cast-iron bar-tracery, of various combinations of circles, segments and straight lines, with a bit of foliage at some of the intersections (Fig. 49). This was much used for the sidelights and for the transoms of doorways, and is still the most striking feature of old city houses. It is often very delicate, pleasing, and richly varied in design. Sometimes this tracery served to hold the glass, but quite often it was independent of it. Its use continued far down into the Greek Revival.

That, in spite of all Dutch influence, English, or rather New England, influences are quite observable, could not be better illustrated than by three Van Renselaer manor houses. Especially noticeable is the tendency to roof elimination. The oldest of these, the one called the "ancient," at Greenbush, New York (Fig. 50), is very quaint and picturesque—Dutch throughout. The hood in Figure 43 belongs to this house. Classic influence is very slight.

But the fine old manor at Albany (Fig. 50), built in 1765, shows Classicism in the ascendency. The roof is a peculiar compromise between the gambrel and the mansard, for what should be the upper slope of the gambrel has become a flat deck, but without producing a mansard, for the end walls are carried up to the full height of the roof. The structure is now being torn down and rebuilt for a college fraternity at Williamstown, Massachusetts. The old Dutch scenic wall paper, which ornamented the hall, has been carefully removed for future use.

In the third manor (Fig. 52), also at Albany, Classic conquest is complete, with strongly marked horizontal lines, a flat roof with a balustrade, an engaged Doric portico, and a Palladian window. This building and the preceding are placed up on high basements, a thing which was rarely done in New England.

Several old mansions are still standing in New York and in its immediate vicinity. Many of these depend for historic interest upon association with Washing-

[6] See also the account of the Verplanck House at Fishkill on Hudson, later on.

- FRONT ELEVATION -

— VAN RENSSELAER MANOR HOUSE —

ALBANY, NEW YORK.

SCALE; 4 FT. TO AN INCH.   BUILT ABOUT A.D. 1790   MEASURED AND DRAWN BY GILBERT F. CRUMP

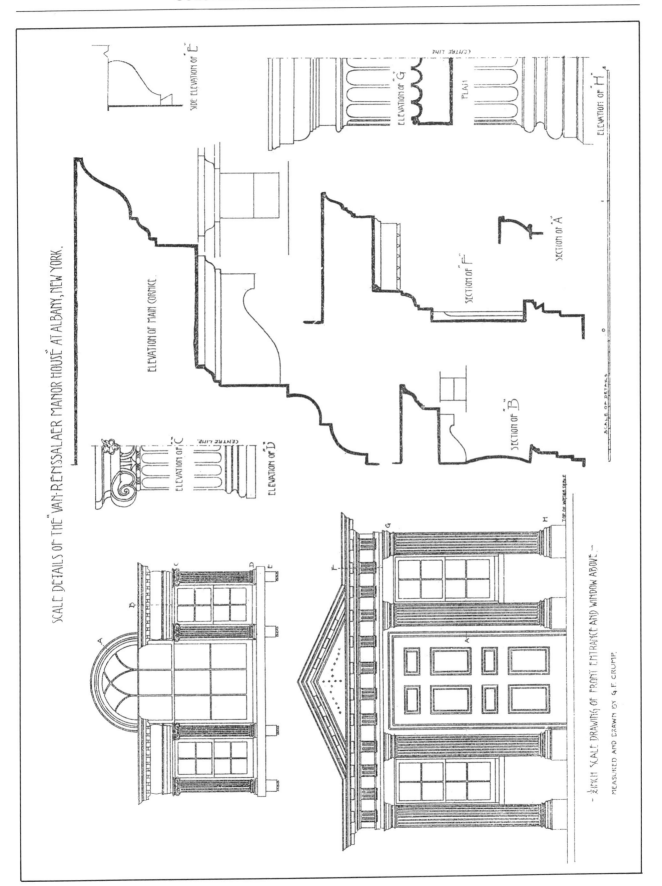

SCALE DETAILS OF THE "VAN-RENSSALAER MANOR HOUSE" AT ALBANY, NEW YORK.

SIDE ELEVATION OF "E"

ELEVATION OF "G"

PLAN

ELEVATION OF "H"

ELEVATION OF MAIN CORNICE.

SECTION OF "F"

SECTION OF "A"

SECTION OF "B"

SCALE OF DETAILS

ELEVATION OF "C"

ELEVATION OF "D"

- ½ INCH SCALE DRAWING OF FRONT ENTRANCE AND WINDOW ABOVE. -

MEASURED AND DRAWN BY G.F. CRUMP.

Fig. 51. MORRIS HOUSE—1762—161ST STREET
AND 10TH AVENUE, NEW YORK CITY

Fig. 52. VAN RENSSELAER
MANOR—1790—ALBANY, NEW YORK

Fig. 53. VAN RENSSELAER MANSION,
ALBANY, NEW YORK

Wings by R. Upjohn, 1840.

Fig. 54. *Marble Mantel*
VAN RENSSELAER MANSION — 1765 — ALBANY,
NEW YORK

ton. Among them is the fine old Jumel mansion at 165th Street and 9th Avenue, built about 1760 (Fig. 55). It has a front porch with very slender two-storied columns. The second-story balcony, under the porch, is carried on cantilevers and extends only half as far as does the main porch. The home of Alexander Hamilton, on the Hamilton Grange, with the thirteen historic elms near by, is also interesting. Its Doric cornice has small inoffensive triglyphs. A balustrade surrounds the flat roof. Two porches only remain of the three which once almost enclosed it upon three sides. No engaged two-story columns or pilasters occur, in fact such features are rare throughout the Middle states, and entirely lacking in the Southern.

Figure 55 represents a little Dutch cottage on 116th Street near Seventh Avenue, New York. It is now almost overgrown with additions and outbuildings — the result of making a "road-house" of it. At present it is used once more as a dwelling. Another and quite similar cottage is illustrated in Figure 42.

Yonker's City Hall might well be called "ancient," as antiquity goes in America. It was built in 1682 by Frederick Philipse for his manor. In 1745 it was considerably enlarged. In 1779, its Tory owner having fled, it was confiscated and sold, only to be rebought in 1868, since which time it has been in use for civic purposes. The structure is rather peculiar, and not very remarkable for beauty. It is long and narrow, two stories high, with a hipped roof relieved by dormers, and crowned by a balustrade running all around the flat deck on top. Upon the long front are two entrances, making it look much as though two houses had grown together.

The Apthorpe House (Fig. 56), which until quite recently existed on the corner of Ninth Avenue and Ninetieth Street, was somewhat peculiar in plan. The plan and elevation were quite similar to that of the home of Washington's mother. Each had a deep two-story recess in the middle. On the front were four two-story pilasters.

The early settlers of Pennsylvania were remarkable in many ways. William Penn prepared upon his immense land grant a refuge for all religious sects. Among these were Quakers, Moravians, Mennonites, Dunkards and Solitary Brethren. In view of such an assemblage of world-eschewing zealots, it is not surprising that Philadelphia is, today, the embodiment of Philistinism.

Many large and often imposing buildings remain, especially in Philadelphia and in Germantown. One of the best of these, a stucco brick structure, somewhat remodeled in later times, is given in Figure 57. Stucco seems to have been largely employed — perhaps owing to German influence — often with brick quoins and other brick trimmings. Stone was, however, the chief building material.

The details generally are hard and crude, and often inappropriate. The home of the colonial botanist, John Bartram, at Philadelphia, built in 1731, has two-story semidetached columns with huge Ionic scrolls. The German rococo mouldings of the window frames, too, are out of all scale with the humble dwelling.

In Pennsylvania there were rarely any verandas, porches, or gardens (Fig. 58). The fierce fight with the primeval forests had engendered a hatred of shade trees: the settlers preferred to let the sun bake their unprotected walls.

The founders of New Sweden in Delaware were too few in numbers to exert any great influence. They, however, introduced an entirely new feature in the construction of frame houses. These they enclosed with upright split palisades, a common mode of building in their native country.

Exceptions are often as interesting as characteristics. If anything can be said to be unique, it surely must be a Protestant convent. Such an one was established by

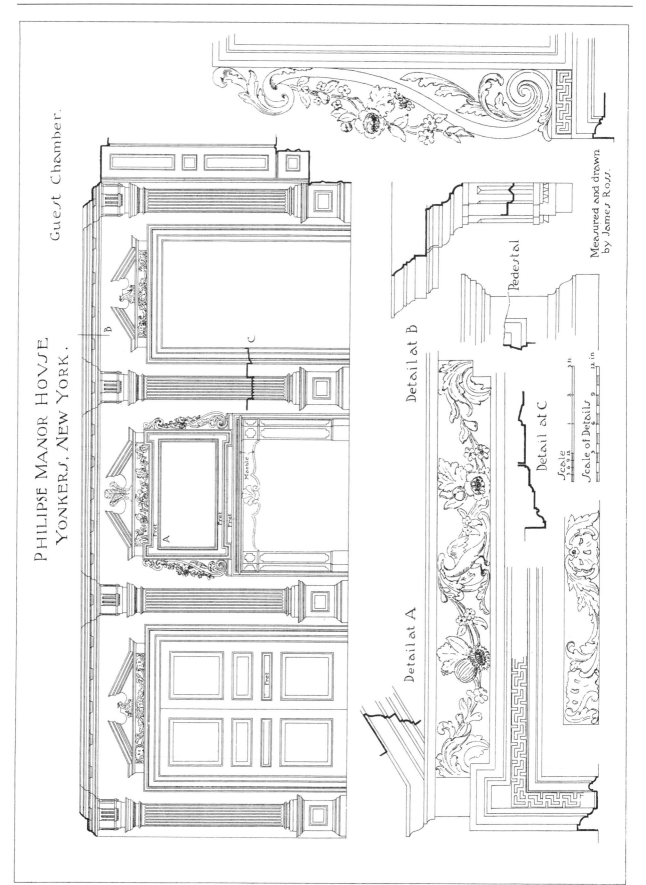

Guest Chamber.

PHILIPSE MANOR HOVSE
YONKERS, NEW YORK.

Detail at A

Detail at B

Detail at C

Pedestal

Measured and drawn
by James Ross.

Scale

Scale of Details

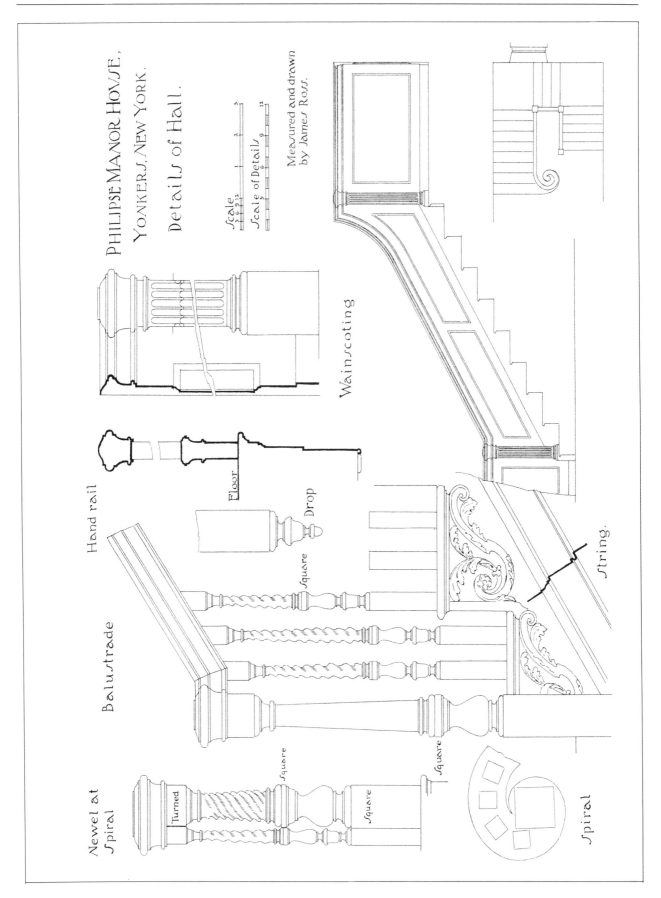

PHILIPSE MANOR HOUSE, YONKERS, NEW YORK.

Details of Hall.

Scale

Scale of Detail

Measured and drawn
by James Ross.

Wainscoting

Hand rail

Floor

Drop

Square

Balustrade

String.

Square

Square

Newel at
Spiral

Turned

Square

Square

Spiral

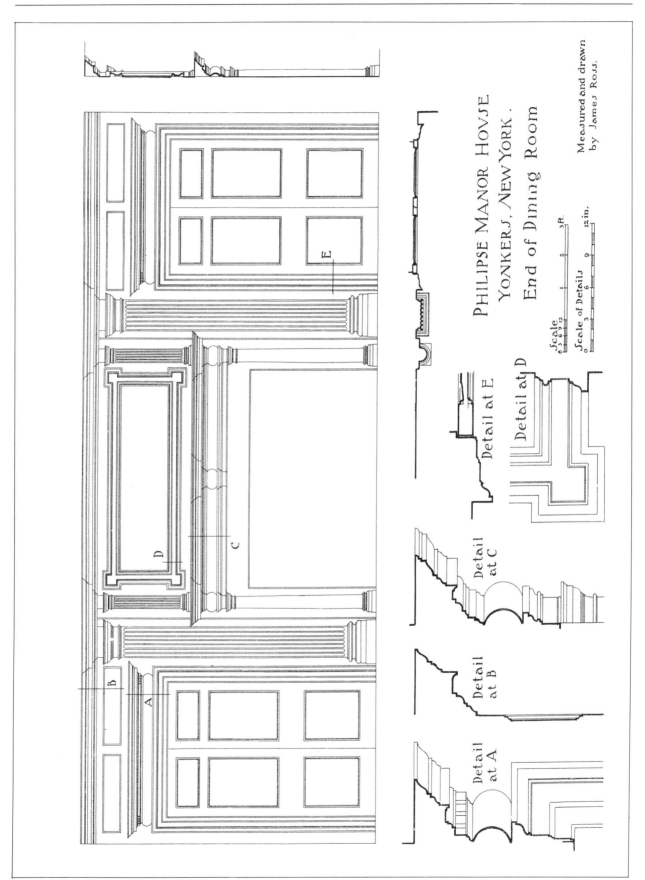

PHILIPSE MANOR HOVSE
YONKERS, NEW YORK.
End of Dining Room

Measured and drawn
by James Ross.

Scale

Scale of Details

Detail at E

Detail at D

Detail at C

Detail at B

Detail at A

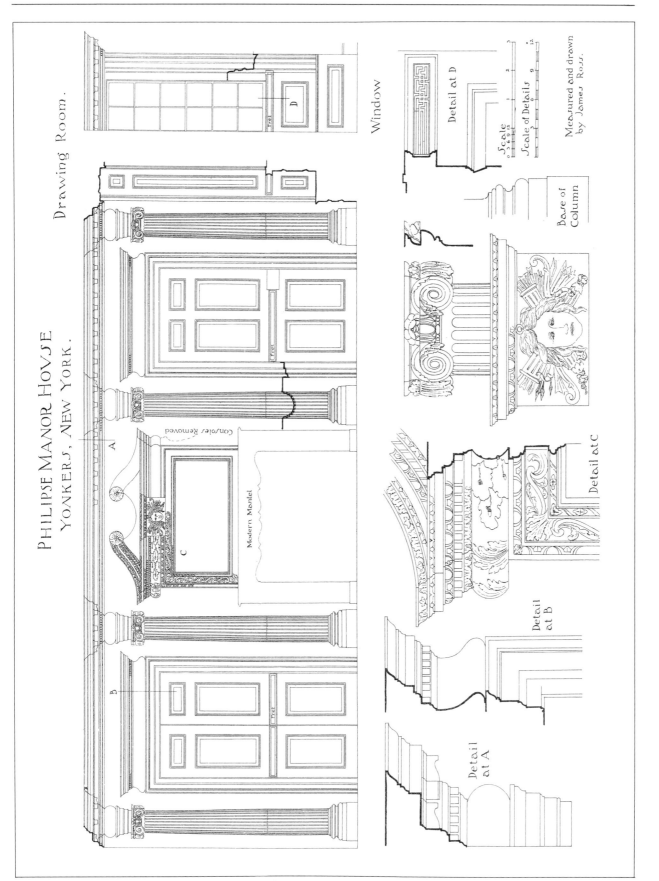

Drawing Room.

Window

Detail at D

Scale

Scale of Details

Measured and drawn by James Ross.

Base of Column

Philipse Manor House
Yonkers, New York.

Consoles Removed

Modern Mantel

Fret

Detail at C

Detail at B

Detail at A

Cornice of South Porch   Cornice over 1st Story Windows

East Elevation
PHILIPSE MANOR HOVSE
YONKERS NEW YORK
Erected about 1745

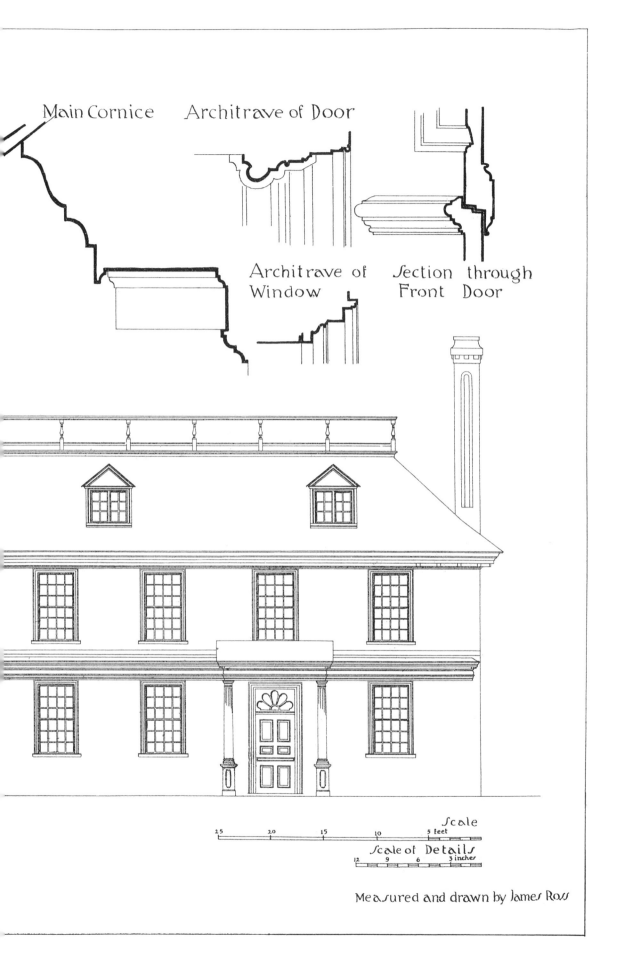

Main Cornice   Architrave of Door

Architrave of   Section through
Window   Front Door

Scale

25   20   15   10   5 feet

Scale of Details

12   9   6   3 inches

Measured and drawn by James Ross

ROCK HALL, LAWRENCE, LONG ISLAND,
NEW YORK

APTHORPE HOUSE, NEW YORK, NEW YORK

Fig. 55. OLD DUTCH COTTAGE, 116TH STREET, NEW YORK CITY, NEW YORK

Fig. 57. COLONIAL HOUSE, GERMANTOWN, PENNSYLVANIA

Fig. 56. APTHORPE HOUSE, 90TH STREET AND 10TH AVENUE, NEW YORK, NEW YORK

Fig. 58. LIVEZEY'S HOUSE, ALLEN'S LANE AND
WISSAHICKON CREEK, PHILADELPHIA
Built 1652 and supposed to be the
oldest house in state.

the so-called Solitary Brethren (and Sisters), in 1725, at Ephrata, near Lancaster, Pennsylvania. This establishment at first grew rapidly in numbers and erected several substantial buildings, some of which are still standing (Fig. 60). These are huge, simple structures, two stories high, with the usual large, steep, German gable. The very small doors and windows, irregularly spaced, produce a gloomy look. The sect, which long ago died out, has been superseded by Seventh Day Baptists.

INTERIORS

Hardly anything can be said of the interiors, so few are illustrated. Scenic wall paper was used somewhat, though only in the best houses. Large wall-paneling of wood was much employed even in ordinary houses. The staircase halls were mostly simple affairs, as in the plan in Figure 55. The hall of the second Van Rensselaer Manor was exceptionally large, 23' x 46', and the stairs were in a separate enclosure off this hall. Some

few staircase halls were very elaborate, as in the Wadsworth House at Genesee, New York, which very much resembled the best work of New England.

In few features was there more uniformity than in the mantels. Many of these from far distant colonies are strikingly similar. It can be said of the greater number of Colonial mantels that they are very pleasing and appropriate in design, and most carefully wrought out in detail. Perhaps they departed more from Classic motives and were less delicate in the Middle colonies than in the other sections. It was quite characteristic of all the mantels to interrupt the frieze below the shelf with an ornamental panel. A similar device was sometimes resorted to in the entablature over the door (Fig. 61).

THE MIDDLE PROVINCES:
PUBLIC ARCHITECTURE

Several notable public buildings, both ecclesiastical and secular, have been preserved. In most of these,

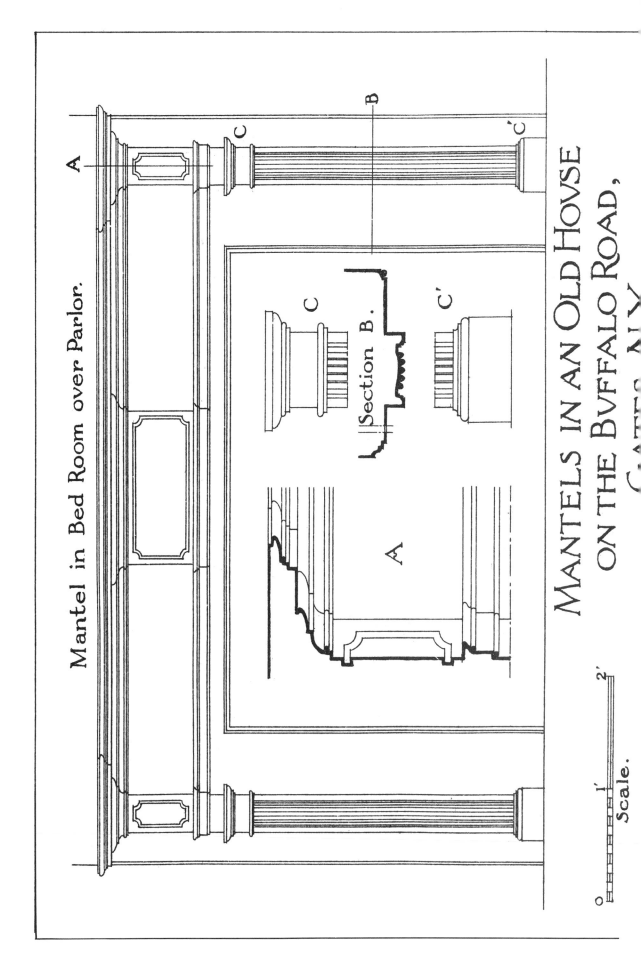

Mantel in Bed Room over Parlor.

Section B.

MANTELS IN AN OLD HOVSE
ON THE BVFFALO ROAD,
GATES, N.Y.

Scale.

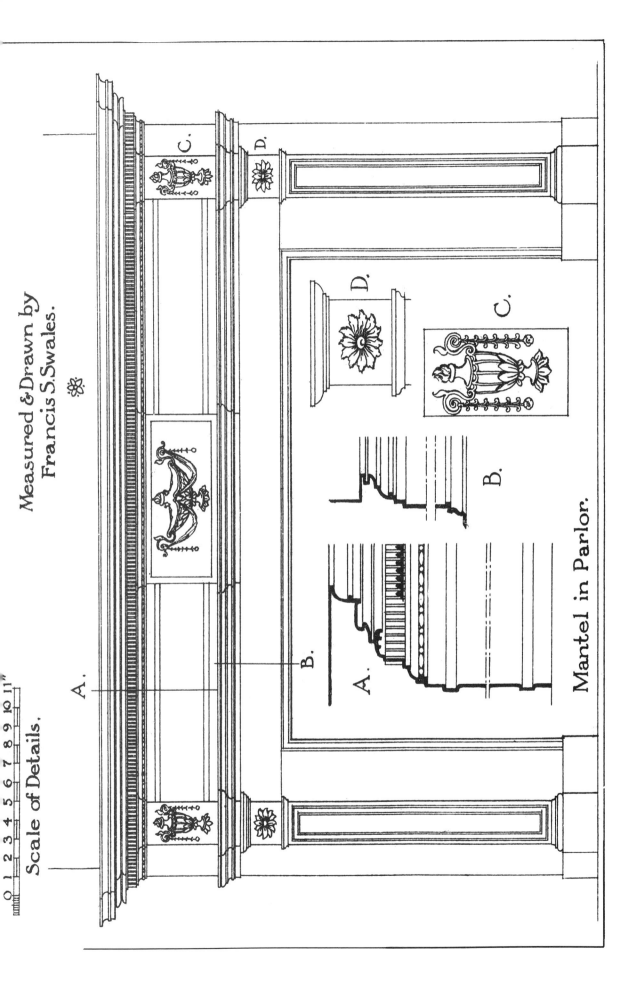

Measured & Drawn by
Francis S. Swales.

Scale of Details.

0 1 2 3 4 5 6 7 8 9 10 11"

A.

B.

C.

D.

Mantel in Parlor.

Fig. 59. "THE MONASTERY," CARPENTER'S
LANE AND WISSAHICKON CREEK,
PHILADELPHIA

English influence is predominant. Traces of Dutch elements, quite marked in the domestic architecture, are here almost entirely wanting. The first structures were Dutch, *e.g.* the old Stadt Huys, or first City Hall, of New York, on the river front, which had stepped gables and other Low Country peculiarities.

First in rank among New York churches is Old Trinity. The present building replaced one which was built in 1788 on the spot where its predecessor, a similar structure, was burned in 1776. This had itself replaced one still older, of which no illustrations have been preserved. The church of 1788 was, as might be expected, somewhat Classical. The entrance porch, semicircular in plan, had four pairs of coupled, Corinthian columns, very much elongated. The six windows on each side were round-arched, but the tower windows, curiously enough, were pointed. There was no effort to make a graceful transition to the octagonal spire—the awkwardness of which was somewhat concealed by a balustrade, with a square pinnacle at each corner. Four similar pinnacles jutted out of the main roof, one at each corner, and eight others continued the lines of the porch columns above the porch cornice. All this gave the church a somewhat Gothic look at a hasty glance.

Two of Trinity's older chapels still exist—both of the Wren type. The one is St. Paul's Chapel, built in 1764–1766. The other is St. John's, half a mile to the northwest, built in 1803–1807. The tower of this latter chapel, once gracing a fashionable neighborhood, now

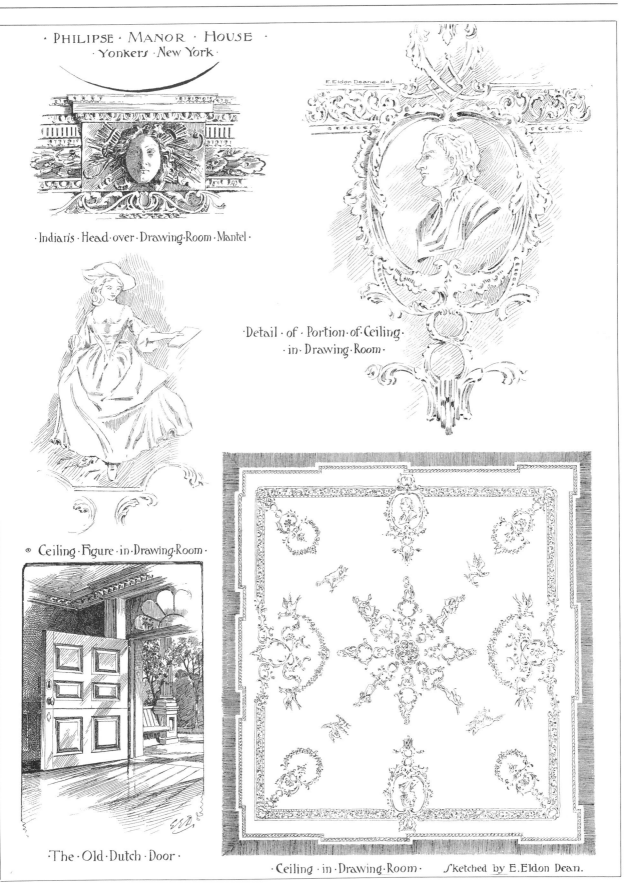

· PHILIPSE · MANOR · HOUSE ·
· Yonkers · New York ·

·Indian's · Head · over · Drawing · Room · Mantel ·

E. Eldon Deane del.

·Detail · of · Portion · of · Ceiling ·
· in · Drawing · Room ·

· Ceiling · Figure · in · Drawing · Room ·

· The · Old · Dutch · Door ·

· Ceiling · in · Drawing · Room ·   Sketched by E. Eldon Dean.

Interior
CHRIST CHURCH — c1720 — PHILADELPHIA,
PENNSYLVANIA
Dr. John Kearsley, Architect

Interior
CHRIST CHURCH — c1720 — PHILADELPHIA,
PENNSYLVANIA
Dr. John Kearsley, Architect

Fig. 60. SAAL AND SARON, EPHRATA, PENNSYLVANIA

frowns down upon Commodore Vanderbilt's freight depot. Perhaps the very squalor and poverty which have overtaken it have been the means of its preservation. The chancel and choir are very effective, each being distinctly marked by the architecture. These two towers are quite similar, both being graceful and slender compositions. St. Paul's is, perhaps, the more pleasing of the two, being more tapering. The churches differ remarkably in their entrance porches: the little two-columned entrance to St. Paul's is just as insignificant as the huge portico of St. John's is colossal and overpowering. John McComb, to whom is ascribed the New York City Hall, is also given as the architect of St. John's Chapel.

The "Brick Church" on Fifth Avenue and Thirty-seventh Street (an enlarged copy[7] of a downtown church, erected in 1767 and long since destroyed), belongs also to the Wren type of churches.

In Philadelphia several remarkable old churches are still to be found. The oldest and largest of these is Christ Church, begun in 1727. It has a large, not ungraceful tower, somewhat of the Wren type, treated, however, without orders. There is no apse—the vista of the interior is closed with a large Palladian window.

This church was designed by Dr. John Kearsley, an amateur architect, and, indeed, he succeeded well. The great fault, however, of this design, as of all Colonial work, is the lack of depth of reveal. No amount of disposition or ornament can satisfy if the whole has

an appearance of being stamped out of sheet metal. It seems strange that the principles of clapboard construction should so thoroughly impress its mark on masonry building. The interior is composed of Doric columns bearing a block of entablature, from which spread the arches.

St. Peter's Church,[8] 1738, also in Philadelphia, has a similar apsidal treatment. Its tower is one of the few not of the Wren type.

Add the Zion Church, and we have three churches of this city with Palladian windows in the gable end.

Hackensack, New Jersey, has a long, low and pleasingly quaint Dutch church, very different from the above. It is a Gothic structure of brownstone, with brick trimmings around the openings, dating from 1696. The pointed windows are probably due rather to a lingering reminiscence of Gothic than to a conscious revival. There are no buttresses or other Gothic features.

In Wilmington, Delaware, there is a small old church, much praised by Mr. White (Fig. 64). He finds the generous side porch particularly charming. Its pleasing lines are no doubt somewhat due to the softening effects of time. This church was erected by the

Fig. 61. *Doorway*—CANANDAIGUA, NEW YORK

---

[7] The present building was erected in 1858.—WARE   [8] See Chapter 3.

Fig. 62. METHODIST EPISCOPAL CHURCH,
WATERLOO, NEW YORK

Fig. 64. OLD STONE [SWEDISH]
CHURCH—1735—WILMINGTON, DELAWARE

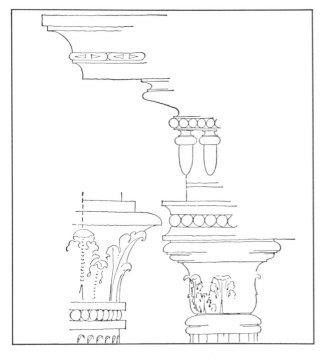

Fig. 63. DETAILS FROM HAMILTON MANSION,
WOODLANDS, NEAR PHILADELPHIA,
PENNSYLVANIA

Swedes in 1735. The still older so-called Old Swedes Church in Philadelphia, built in 1700, is very similar, and there are others.

Two civic buildings of New York City deserve special mention. They are the little Sub-Treasury Building on Wall Street and its near and important relative, the City Hall. The latter is too well known to require many words (Plan, Fig. 65). Its architect is said to have been John McComb (1763–1853) born in New York. He was an ardent admirer of Sir Wm. Chambers's, but was also influenced by the brothers Adam. But some wish to credit this building to a certain Mangin, an itinerant French draughtsman employed by McComb. The work of construction lasted from 1803 to 1812. The entire cost was not fully half a million dollars. It is built of marble on three sides, and is, in execution, an advance over earlier buildings in mechanical perfection as well as in monumental design. But even this structure partakes of the Colonial cardboard appearance. This building is undoubtedly the second best, largest and the last important production of the period under consideration. It is a pity that its style was to be swamped by the Greek Revival at a time when it seemed still to possess vitality. Its predecessor on Wall

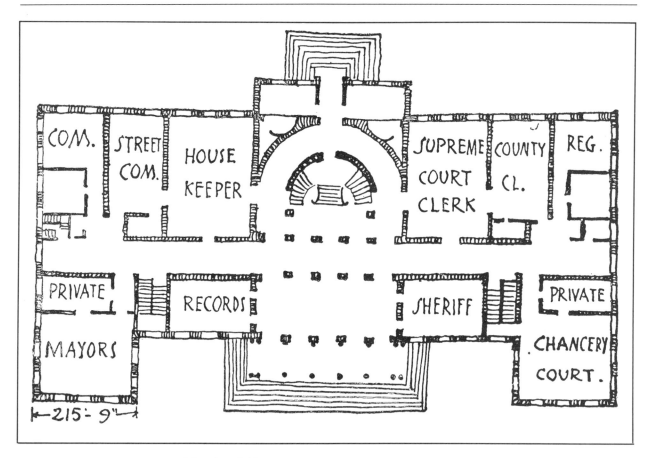

Fig. 65. CITY HALL—1803—NEW YORK CITY,
NEW YORK
J. McComb, Architect

Fig. 66. STATE HOUSE, OR INDEPENDENCE
HALL—1735—PHILADELPHIA, PENNSYLVANIA
Andrew [or James] Hamilton, Architect

Street was a comparatively mean affair with the inevitable cupola straddling the roof-ridge.

The state house, or the so-called Independence
Hall, at Philadelphia, built in 1735, is, perhaps, from a
sentimental point-of-view, the most important building that we possess from colonial times (Fig. 66). It has
lately been restored to its condition in 1776 and
presents strong southern affinities, in having a wing on
each side, like Figure 69, connected with a lower portion, as well as in its general long low lines. The details
of the interior are quite good and Classical; marred,
however, by some bizarre attempts at innovation. Its
architect was James (?) Hamilton, also an amateur
architect, whose professional training was that of a
lawyer.

To the category of public structures must, also, be
added King's College Building, New York, Trinity's
foster child. In 1756, the trustees erected this "lime-
house," 30′ x 180′, on the Trinity land grant, bounded
by Church, Murray and Barclay streets and by the
river, a site described as being "in the suburbs." The
design was quite severe, even factory-like, three stories

high on a low basement. Four slight projections with steep pediments varied the front. The windows and doorways were plain. The hipped roof was flat on top, with a balustrade running all around it. An octagonal cupola, the stock-in-trade with colonial builders, supported the famous copper crown. This building was in use just about one hundred years.

Taverns have played an important part in New York's history. The old Dutch custom of discussing all matters over a pot seems to have continued far down into the seventeenth century. The cumbrous, and often dangerous, signboards were striking features. Bull's Head Tavern is the one most frequently illustrated (Fig. 68). The old Fraunces Tavern still stands on Broad and Pearl streets.

The "Father of American Libraries," at Philadelphia, and predecessor of the present Ridgway Library, built its first home in 1790. It is a rather insignificant,

two-story structure with a low hipped roof. In the middle of the front are four tall Ionic columns, with full entablature and pediment. Only the cornice of this entablature continues around the building.

The Capitol in the city of Washington was the most important and largest building undertaken, as was eminently proper. In its design and erection are involved several names. Here, too, we meet with the amateur architect. Dr. William Thornton submitted in competition, 1793, the most acceptable plans. These were revised by Hallet, a Frenchman. James Hoban, an Irishman, was superintendent of construction and for a time did some of the designing. In 1795 George Hadfield, an English architect, was appointed. In 1803 Latrobe became architect. In 1817 he was succeeded by Charles Bulfinch, the Boston architect, who completed the structure in 1830. Its size was 121' x 355'. The dome measured 120 feet to the top.

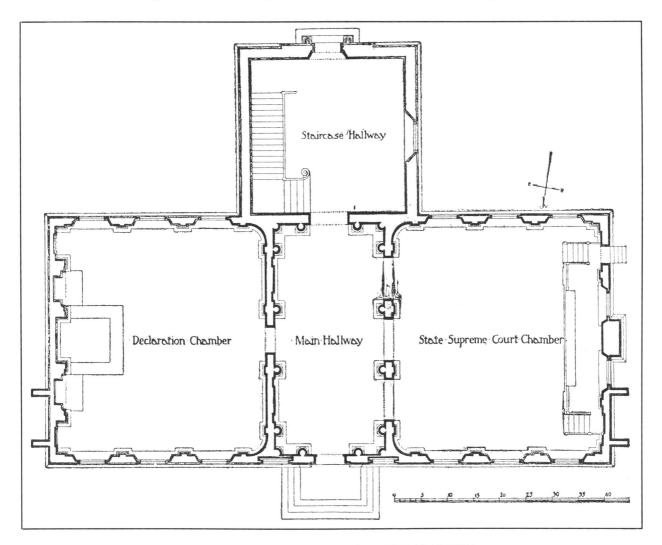

Fig. 67. INDEPENDENCE HALL, PHILADELPHIA, PENNSYLVANIA

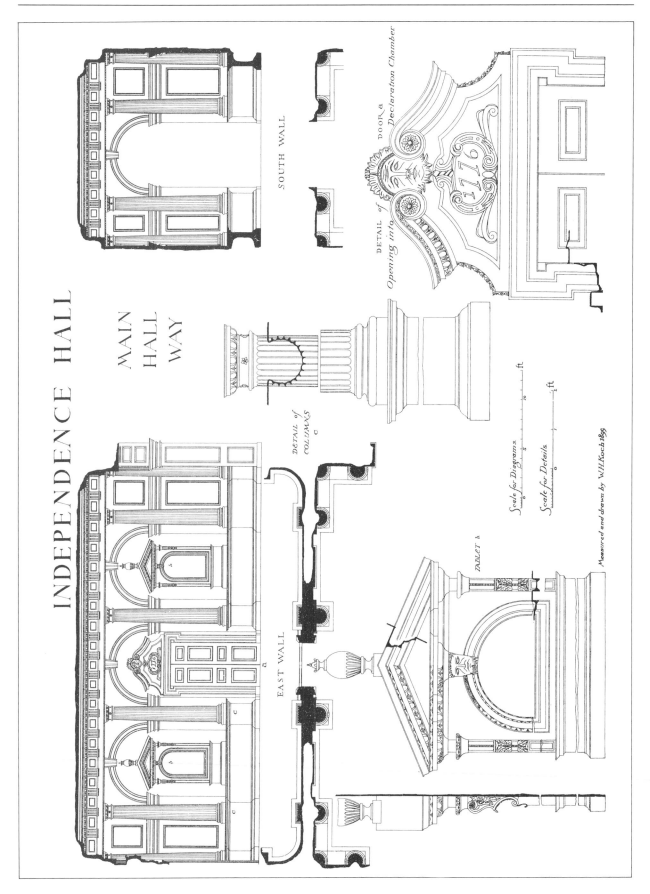

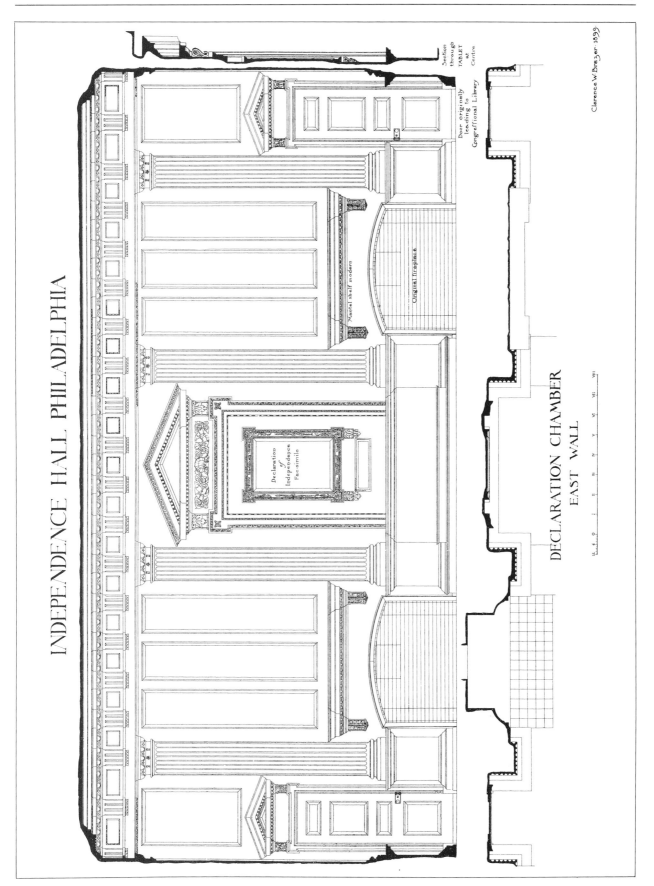

INDEPENDENCE HALL PHILADELPHIA

DECLARATION CHAMBER
EAST WALL

Section
through
TABLET
at
Centre

Door originally
leading to
Congressional Library

Clarence W. Brazer 1899

Mantel shelf modern

Original fireplace

Declaration
of
Independence
Fac-simile

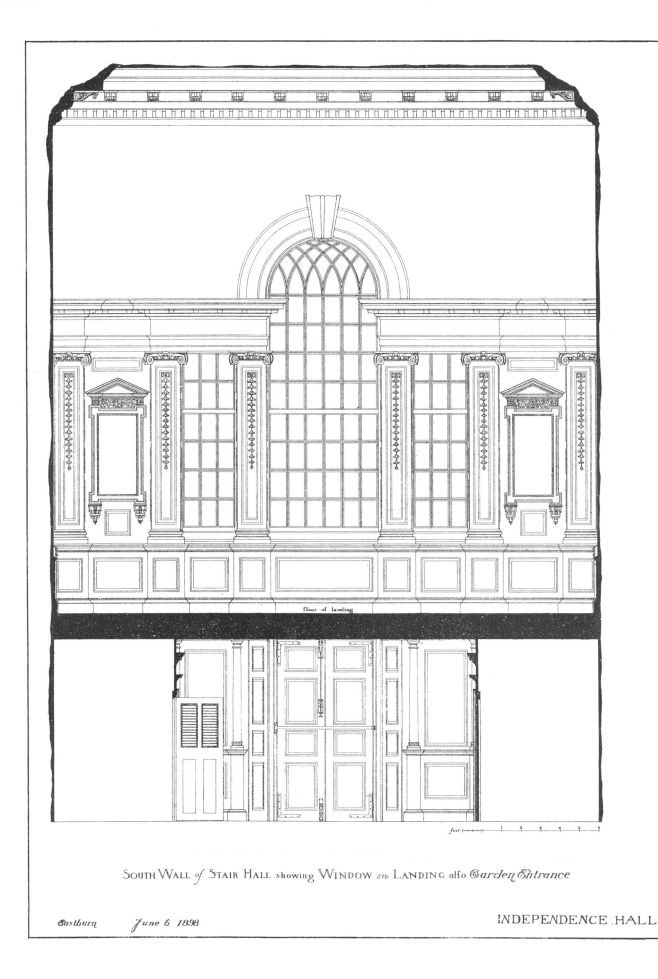

floor of landing

feet

SOUTH WALL of STAIR HALL showing WINDOW on LANDING also *Garden Entrance*

Eastburn   *June 6 1898*

INDEPENDENCE HALL

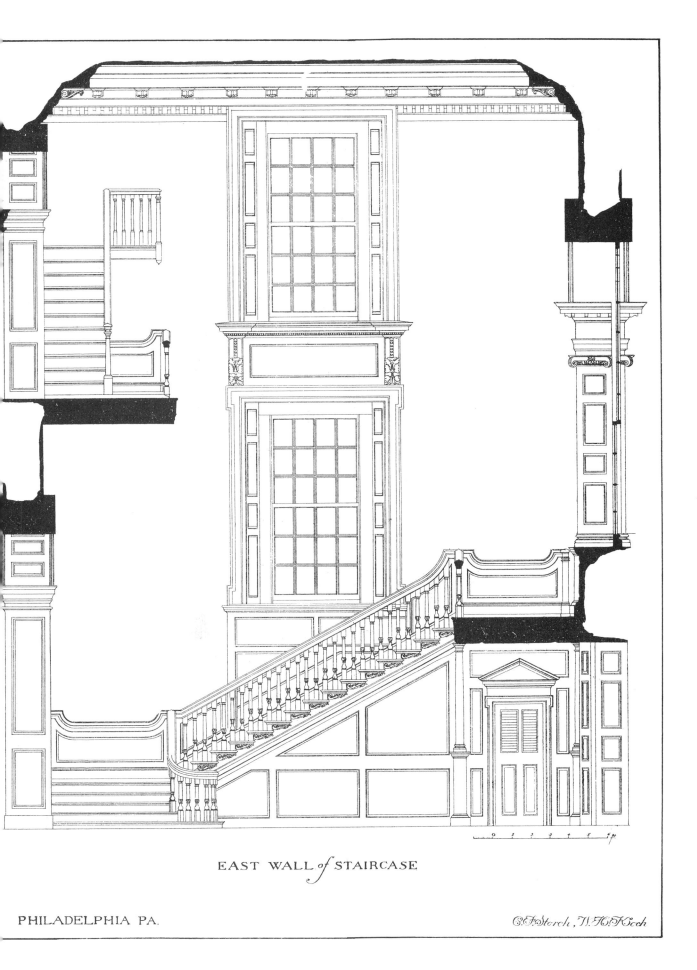

EAST WALL *of* STAIRCASE

PHILADELPHIA PA.

C.F.Storch, W.H.Koch

Fig. 68. OLD BULL'S HEAD TAVERN,
NEW YORK CITY, NEW YORK

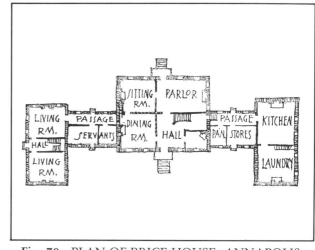

Fig. 70. PLAN OF BRICE HOUSE, ANNAPOLIS,
MARYLAND

This now magnificent pile was a fitting close of the Colonial work and exemplified the best elements. Monumental, massive and well proportioned, it is a credit to the country and to its designers.

Although the study of the architecture of the Middle Provinces has not been without interest, it has on the whole been rather unsatisfactory. There were too many and too various elements. No unity could result in so short a time; no distinct style was evolved; few single new features, even, were produced. All this was quite different in New England, as we have seen. So it was in the Old Dominion. The peculiarities of a Massachusetts or of a Virginia mansion are so marked as to be readily distinguished. But a house in the Middle colonies might as well have been built in England, in Holland, in Germany, in Sweden, or in some other part of colonial America. Moreover, this section has almost been overlooked by writers and investigators, probably on account of its comparative lack of interest.

THE SOUTHERN PROVINCES: DOMESTIC ARCHITECTURE

In the Southern colonies, in the land of romance, we encounter many new elements. The aristocratic cavaliers who settled there differed in much from the Puritans. Their religion was that of the Church of England. Their slaves were mostly black men, and were employed in the raising of tobacco, the staple product. "Essentially a countryman by preference, he [the cavalier planter] loved, above all things, the comparative solitude of a great country home, with its dependent village of servants, farm-hands and mechanics, its stables full of English horses, its barns filled with high-bred cattle, and, beyond, its flourishing fields of tobacco and grain."

Roads in this country were mere bridle paths. The traders were peddlers; the artisans were tinkers. Commerce was thought unbefitting a gentleman. The soil

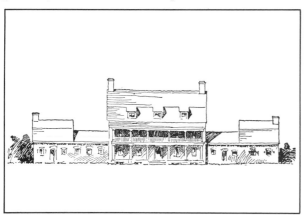

Fig. 69. OLD MANOR HOUSE, MARYLAND

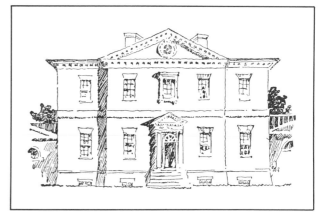

Fig. 71. HARWOOD HOUSE — 1770 —
ANNAPOLIS, MARYLAND

Fig. 72. *Pediment Window*
HARWOOD HOUSE, ANNAPOLIS, MARYLAND

Fig. 73. *Rear Door*
TULIP HILL — 1750 — WEST RIVER, MARYLAND

Fig. 74. TULIP HILL — 1750 — WEST RIVER,
MARYLAND

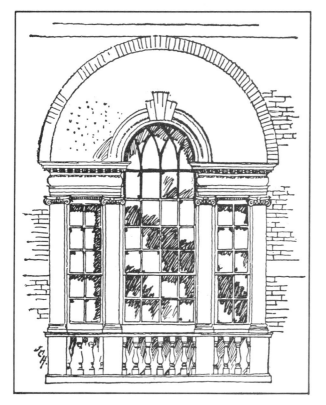

Fig. 75. FROM THE CHASE HOUSE — 1770 —
ANNAPOLIS, MARYLAND

and Brandon, built in 1790. In Maryland is the Severn, at the mouth of which lies charming Annapolis. Others of some note are Goose Creek in South Carolina, and West River, the York and the Potomac in Virginia, all of which, and many others, served as highways of travel.

Towns were few; cities almost none. Jamestown, the first attempt at a settlement in Virginia, had a short life. Its few remaining ruins are now rapidly crumbling. Williamsburg, which superseded it, never became important — it stands today, with a church and a court house, almost the identical country town it was a hundred years ago.

Annapolis in Maryland is exceptional. It is indeed fortunate that so complete and beautiful a little city as this has been preserved. Considerate Progress left it to its colonial glory and built up Baltimore. The older Maryland town is remarkable in many ways. Its streets radiate from two circular plazas. Upon the larger of these were the buildings of the State, upon the smaller those of the Church — pivotal points of social organization. Business blocks and tradesmen's houses were confined by law within a fixed quarter near the dock. The many fine residences, some close up to the street, others setting back, were generally placed in large gardens sloping towards the river. From the upper win-

was very fertile, so that the planters were soon enabled to indulge in a lavish hospitality, which, however, often proved ruinous. The uncertain value of tobacco, which fluctuated from year to year, also tempted to live above means.

Owing to the origin of many of the settlers, some of whom were sons of prominent English noblemen, there was from the beginning much taste and refinement. Thus the Virginia gentry were the first to introduce glass for the lighting of rooms. Comfortable and substantial houses were built very early. Perhaps the inherited desire of the Virginia settler to live in dignity and splendor can best explain his preference for brick, in a country where wood was the most natural material, and where it was everywhere abundant. Many old and lordly manors lie scattered along the rivers, mute witnesses of past glory.

The rivers were the only safe and practicable highways. For this reason, and for purposes of commerce, each planter fought to have his own riverfront, with a little dock to which the small Dutch and New England vessels would come for barter. The James River in Virginia, often spoken of as the "Classic James," is the best known. Some of the important manors along this river are: Shirley, built in 1700; Westover, built in 1737; Carter's Grove Hall (Fig. 78) built in the same year;

Fig. 76. *Front Gate*
WESTOVER, ON THE JAMES, VIRGINIA

Fig. 77. *Fenceposts*
WESTOVER, ON JAMES RIVER, VIRGINIA

dows a fine view was obtained down the terraces to the wooded brink. This little "Queen Anne" city possessed not only civic buildings, churches and schools, but also clubhouses, a theatre, and a racecourse. Its prosperity began about 1750, and lasted only down to the Revolution.

Log houses were built only at the very outset. Here, too, the puncheon floor was the first improvement. Frame houses must have been rare. Some are spoken of, but none have been found worthy of illustration. The Southerner, considering wood a poor building material, did not discover the good use to which clapboards and shingles can be put. Bricks seemed to him to be the only material to be employed in a structure of any importance. Even minor structures, servants' quarters and outbuildings, such as barns (Fig. 82), and dove-cotes (Fig. 79), were generally of brick. In the earlier days the bricks were imported, stowed away as ballast in returning ships. This, however, was too slow and expensive, and soon they were burned on the spot, good clay and fuel being abundant.

Flemish bond was most commonly used by bricklayers. In many instances the alternating bricks were of a darker color, sometimes even glazed. The device of laying all the bricks headers, as done in the Jennings House, Annapolis, is very unsatisfactory, the bond apparently being weaker than when all are laid stretchers.

There is marked individuality in the planning, on account of the many smaller structures required by the large estates with their hosts of dependants. In Maryland, the offices, servants' quarters, tool-houses and the like, were built as story-and-a-half wings connected with the main part by one-story corridors (Figs. 69, 70). In Virginia, on the other hand, isolation was preferred, and these secondary structures, though low, were often two stories in height. This practice, however, was not without exceptions.

Generally the plans were symmetrical—a wing on one side balanced by one on the other, with the entrance in the middle. In Virginia this opened upon a hall running right through. Shirley manor is an exception, and is said to have a French mediaeval prototype. In this building, 50' x 80', the hall is in the northwestern corner. Similar planning was quite common in Annapolis, in which place many other traces of French influence are found. In the Chase House, at Annapolis, the rooms are arranged also upon a transverse axis.

The plan being symmetrical, it was only natural that a like disposition should be found in the façade. In the Harwood House, Annapolis (Fig. 71), the axis of the front is well marked by the doorway of the first story, by a splendid window above and by a rich bull's-eye in the attic. A detail of this attic window is given in Figure 72. The slight projection of the middle part, with a pediment over, is common in Annapolis. In this case, however, it is entirely unwarranted by the interior arrangements.

Ornamental wall pilasters or semidetached columns never occur on these brick structures. The nearest approach to them is found under porches, where they

Fig. 78. CARTER'S GROVE, JAMES RIVER, VIRGINIA

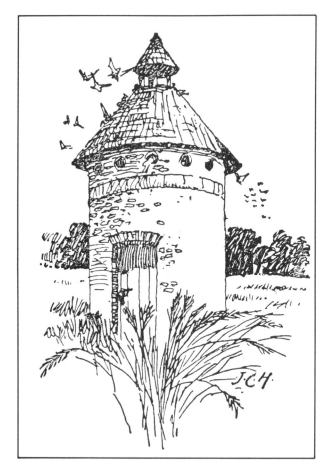

Fig. 79. PIGEON HOUSE, JAMES RIVER,
VIRGINIA

exceptional. It was employed on the huge pile of Rose-well, three stories high and ninety feet square. The construction of this manor and a too lavish hospitality involved its owner in so deep a debt that his son and successor had to apply for permission to sell a part of the estate—the English law of entail being strictly observed. Rosewell has since been standing tenantless for a century, no owner being wealthy enough to keep it up.

Dormers were not very common, and were but little varied in design. Balustrades were never used upon the roof and occur rarely anywhere. The roof covering was ordinarily of tin, standing-seam joint: slates and shingles were also sometimes used.

The entrances were treated, much as in the other colonies, with a flanking order supporting a pediment. Over the door there is usually a transom, but sidelights are almost entirely wanting. A rather ingenious variation of the shell hood is given in Figure 73, from Maryland.

Palladian windows were rare. The fine example from the Chase House (Fig. 75), once before referred to, is quite unique. Other windows are very simple, usually mere openings in the wall with flat brick arches above. The two central windows of the Harwood House (Fig. 71) are exceptionally elaborate. The woodwork of the doors and windows, as indeed all the other wooden trim, was painted white so as to set off against the deep red of the bricks.

But little space can be devoted to the accessories, some of which are quite elaborate and well studied. Westover, on the James River, possesses three beauti-

Fig. 80. *Stair String*
CARTER'S GROVE—1737—VIRGINIA

are used as responds to the free-standing columns. Porches, however, are rare; in the earlier buildings they were entirely wanting. Some were added later, as the settlers learned the exigencies of the climate. The disposition of the columns is very simple, with little attempt at variety. The Annapolis porches were, mostly, mere little entrance stoops; often there were none at all. Perhaps the brick walls, from two or three feet thick, afforded an ampler protection against the hot fun than did the frame enclosures of New England.

Two-story porches, such as that in Figure 69, occur in some instances. Gov. Bull Pringle's mansion in South Carolina has a somewhat similar porch. Some few examples very like the characteristic Connecticut porches (Fig. 17) are also to be seen.

The buildings were rarely more than two stories high, with low, hipped roofs. Some of the earlier structures, as Westover (built in 1737), had very steep roofs. In a few instances the end walls were carried up with a huge chimney rising out of the ridge. The gambrel roof was not used at all, and the flat roof was

Fig. 81. SCOTT HOUSE — 1780 — ANNAPOLIS, MARYLAND

ful wrought iron gates. The best one of these is illustrated in Figure 76. Hardly any single feature could be cited better to illustrate the wealth and taste of its nabob owner. These gates were of course imported from England, all the handicrafts, especially in the South, being still in their infancy.

Figure 77, illustrating the tops of two fenceposts at Westover, shows the care and attention given even to very small matters.

Many gardens, especially in Annapolis, must have been splendid in their prime, laid out as some of them were supposed to be "after the Italian manner," with statuary, shrubbery, paths and sloping terraces. So, too, in the less poetic matter of outbuildings the charming dove-cote at Shirley (Fig. 79) shows its owner's careful consideration and preference for substantiality in all things.

Here, as in New England, the halls were made into sumptuous features. That at Carter's Grove is twenty-eight feet wide, or one-third of the entire floor area. A fine arch, on wall columns, usually divides the front part of the hall from the rear, which contains the stairs. These are in three runs, the steps broad and easy, with three balusters, each different, for every tread (Fig. 80). The rail ends in a scroll at the bottom, with the last balluster, more elaborate than the others, spirally carved (Fig. 84). Mahogany was used in the best examples.

The walls were wainscoted in wood up to the ceilings in large panels, though sometimes plaster panels were used. The ceilings were often decorated in delicate plaster relief, in a somewhat rococo style. The cornice was of many members, often with rich modil-

lions. In the Chase House the frieze is decorated with a fine Greek wave motive.

From these cool, wind-swept halls two views could be obtained — in the one direction, down the terraces to the placid river, in the other, up the rising plantation to the wooded hills beyond.

The steps were in some instances of solid timbers projecting from the wall, each resting on the one below. A similar device, borrowed from stone construction, was used in one of the colonial country-houses in New York State (Fig. 86). One might reasonably expect less of lightness and caprice, and more of solidity and formality in the details and finish of a house with brick walls two or three feet thick than in one with a six or eight inch frame enclosure. This expectation is partly justified. The mantelpieces, many of them of white or variegated marble, were quite simple and Classic in design, as may be seen in Figure 85, a very beautiful piece of work. Croisettes and egg-and-dart mouldings seem to have been the main elements of design; some very elaborate rococo mantels harmonizing well with the other details of the room, are found in Annapolis. Slender, graceful mantels in wood, with a wealth of hand-carved flutes and beads are by no means wanting. They are usually, as in Figure 87, further enriched by a putty decoration of delicate modeling. Pictured Dutch tiles do not occur — the cavaliers did not come to America by way of Holland.

The door and window trims are quite Classical. Often they show marked French influence, as in Figures 83, 90 and 91, which have very different merit in design. Figure 90, remarkably beautiful in itself, looks weak and inappropriate as the base of an architrave.

Fig. 82. *Stable* — 1780 — HOMEWOOD, MARYLAND

Fig. 83. *Door Head* — WHITEHALL, MARYLAND

Fig. 85. WESTOVER — 1737 — ON THE JAMES, VIRGINIA

Fig. 84. *Stair Balustrade*
CARTER'S GROVE, ON THE JAMES, VIRGINIA

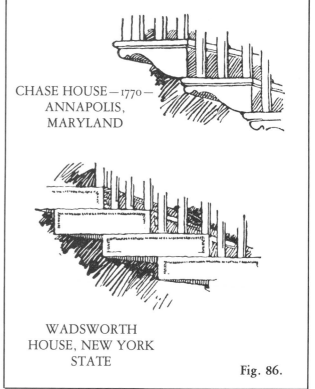

CHASE HOUSE — 1770 —
ANNAPOLIS,
MARYLAND

WADSWORTH
HOUSE, NEW YORK
STATE

Fig. 86.

Fig. 87. CAZANOVE—c1806—ALEXANDRIA, VIRGINIA

Niches, common enough decorative devices in Europe, occur rarely in Colonial work. In the upper hall of the Chase House are two which balance one another, at the head of the stairs (Fig. 92). The niche was, however, commonly adapted to the useful purpose of a cupboard (Fig. 93). Similar treatment with shell carving occurred in New England (Fig. 28).

SOUTHERN PUBLIC ARCHITECTURE: SECULAR BUILDINGS

We have seen that few public buildings were required in New England: still fewer are to be found in the Southern colonies with their small and sparse settlements. Excepting the churches, which are mostly unpretentious and commonplace, there are hardly any public structures to be discussed.

The names of some designers have been handed down, among which is that of the illustrious Wren. To

Fig. 88. *Mantel*—WILLIAMSBURG, VIRGINIA

him are attributed, with perhaps scant foundation in fact, the court house and the first buildings for William and Mary College at Williamsburg, Virginia. The court house (Fig. 94) is a simple little structure, not unpleasing, though looking rather much like a schoolhouse, in spite of, or perhaps rather in consequence of, the indispensable cupola. The absence of porch columns, which seems to have been a part of the original design, is very striking.

The State House and St. John's College of Annapolis are quite large and very similar. Each is unfortunate in its badly proportioned dome, which we would like to believe to be later additions. In other respects they have the Colonial characteristics. The customhouse at Charleston, South Carolina (Fig. 95), is also a pleasing structure, well expressing its civic destination. It has historic interest from its use as a prison during the Revolution.

The versatile Thomas Jefferson is to be found also among the designers. As an amateur architect he may be said to have been unusually successful. The University of Virginia, of which he was both founder and architect, is his best known work. It is, perhaps, the first structure in America in which the dome was used as an important exterior and interior feature (Figs. 89,

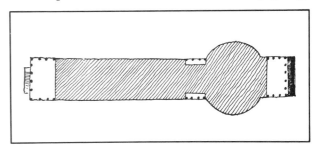

Fig. 89. UNIVERSITY OF VIRGINIA, CHARLOTTESVILLE, VIRGINIA

96). The buildings enclose three sides of a quadrangle 200' x 600'. They cost the great sum of $300,000, an immense amount for those times. The group exhibits, as do few, if any, contemporary Colonial works, an appreciation of monumental planning in its large, simple and well-defined masses. Much of it has lately been rebuilt and added to by the architects McKim, Mead & White, of New York, since the fire of 1894, which came near destroying this very interesting composition.

Two domestic structures are ascribed to Jefferson: Farmington and his own Monticello both near Charlotteville, Virginia. The construction and the embellishment of Monticello brought him to bankruptcy during the last days of his life.

Jefferson had a preference for colossal columns. He employed all of the five orders, but confined himself

Wrought Iron Newels and Railings
VARICK STREET, NEW YORK, NEW YORK

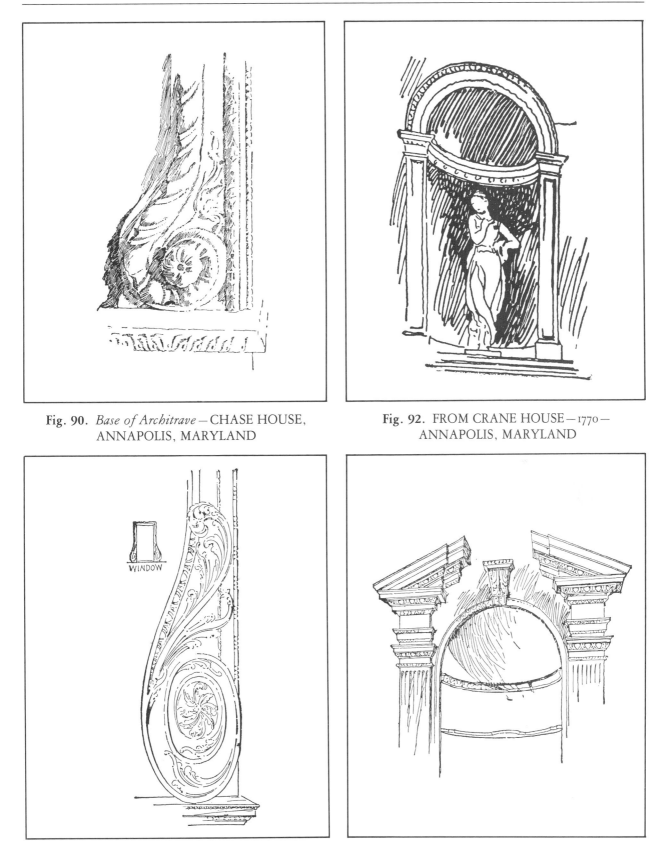

Fig. 90. *Base of Architrave* — CHASE HOUSE, ANNAPOLIS, MARYLAND

Fig. 92. FROM CRANE HOUSE — 1770 — ANNAPOLIS, MARYLAND

Fig. 91. *Base of Architrave* — WHITEHALL, VIRGINIA

Fig. 93. FROM GUNSTON HALL — 1757 — VIRGINIA

Detail of Mantel
HOUSE ON SOUTH THIRD STREET,
PHILADELPHIA, PENNSYLVANIA

Detail of Mantel

HOUSE ON SOUTH THIRD STREET,
PHILADELPHIA, PENNSYLVANIA

Fig. 94. COURT HOUSE — c1700 —
WILLIAMSBURG, VIRGINIA
Sir C. Wren, Architect

mostly to the Doric. He made a conscious and studious effort to "do the proper thing" in the Italian Renaissance style, including the laying out of gardens with all manner of accessories. But in spite of this he did many queer things. One conceit was the ornamentation of the drawing room frieze, which consisted of ox skulls, vases, tomahawks, rosettes, warclubs, scalping knives and the like. Another was a combination of dumbwaiter and fireplace.

Jefferson was a man of some mechanical ingenuity, and he invented many interesting and useful appliances. At the University he attempted to build a brick wall four feet high and only four inches, or one brick, thick. To do this and make it stable, he built it in a waving line, somewhat after the manner of a split-rail fence.

The capitol of Virginia at Richmond is also in a measure due to Jefferson's energies. The design is by M. Clarissault, a French architect considered for his day "most correct." The building measures 70' x 134'.

But little that is new can be said of the few churches which remain and are illustrated. In all the public architecture there was far less of individuality and of interest than in private work. Tradition tells that St. Luke's Church, Newport Parish, Virginia, was built in 1632, or even two years before the Cradock House mentioned in the beginning of this paper. But this is hardly credible, though it must be very old. It is 30' x 50', with a tower 18 feet square, 50 feet high, without offsets. It has coupled pointed windows and buttresses. The doorway is round arched. There are

brick quoins on the angles. This old building has lately been restored.

St. Michael's Church, at Charleston, South Carolina, [1752], seems to have been one of the largest and most pretentious. It has a Doric portico of four colossal columns. Its large Wren-like tower is rather ungainly, tapering awkwardly, and insufficiently crowned by a stumpy spire. Its size is 58' x 80', the spire 192 feet high. It was built from designs imported from England. St. Phillip's, also of Charleston, was built in 1733, thus being somewhat older, in size 62' x 74', but in many other respects similar.

All that remains of the ruined church in old Jamestown is the base of the tower, now almost overgrown with gnarled trees, and looking dismal and forlorn in the low swamps. It has been a favorite subject with the hunter after the picturesque.

On Goose Creek, in South Carolina, is another interesting ruin (Fig. 97). The interior, still in a fair condition, with well-preserved frescos, possess a rather fine pulpit, resembling somewhat the one in King's Chapel, Boston, previously referred to.

The Williamsburg church, in Figure 99, is a large plain structure. A traveling Englishman described it one hundred years ago as an "indifferent church." He

Fig. 95. CUSTOMHOUSE — 1752 — CHARLESTON,
SOUTH CAROLINA

Fig. 96. UNIVERSITY OF VIRGINIA — 1817 — CHARLOTTESVILLE, VIRGINIA

Fig. 98. ST. JOHN'S CHURCH — 1660–1667 — HAMPTON, VIRGINIA

was right, but Time has softened its hard lines, partly covered it with green, and otherwise tinted it with soft and mellow tones from his varied palette.

The other Virginia churches, illustrated in Bishop Meade's *Old Churches, Ministers, and Families of Virginia,* are all of slight interest. The best one is given in Figure 98. The Southern gentry were not very churchy, and it is hardly to be expected that they would have left us any remarkable structures.

have served to show that there was in that section much building activity. The manors of the planters have been less disturbed than have the houses of the New England builders. Progress, that friend and destroyer in one, has passed them by. The South received a greater setback in the Revolution than did the North. Then came the Civil War. It is only lately that some of the estates are beginning to rally. A few have been put in shape; fences have been rebuilt and the fields once more bear harvests. Others still lie desolate. From all, the spirit of the old cavaliers has fled as completely as has the spirit of Puritanism from New England. But the South is waking up and prosperity, with its train of attendants, is returning to the Old Dominion.

Fig. 97. ST. JAMES'S CHURCH — 1711 — GOOSE CREEK, SOUTH CAROLINA

Fig. 99. CHRIST CHURCH, WILLIAMSBURG, VIRGINIA

CAPEN HOUSE — 1810 — BINGHAMTON,
NEW YORK

CAPEN HOUSE — 1810 — BINGHAMTON,
NEW YORK

Rear View
OLD STONE HOUSE, GUILFORD,
CONNECTICUT

THE OLD STONE HOUSE AT GUILFORD, CONNECTICUT

"This house was erected by the Rev. Henry Whitfield, both for the accommodation of his family and as a fortification for the protection of the inhabitants against the Indians. It is the oldest stone dwelling-house now standing in New England. This house was kept in its original form until 1868, when it underwent such renovation as to change to some extent its interior arrangement, although the north wall and large stone chimney are substantially the same as they have been for over two centuries. It is said that the first Guilford marriage was celebrated in it, the wedding-table being garnished with pork and pease. According to tradition, the stone of which this house was built was brought by the Indians on hand-barrows across a swamp from Griswold rock, a ledge about eighty rods east of the house. It consisted of two stories and an attic. The walls were 3 feet thick. At the southeast corner of the second floor there was a singular embrasure commanding the approach from the south and west, and evidently made for defensive purposes. In the attic were two recesses, evidently intended as places of concealment." — Smith's *History of Guilford.*

The following description, taken from Volume 2 of Palfrey's *History of New England*, gives other details: —

"The walls are of stone from a ledge eighty rods distant to the east. It was probably brought on hand-barrows across a swamp over a rude causeway, which is still to be traced. A small addition has in modern times been made to the back of the house, but there is no question but the main building remains in its original state, even to the oak of the beams, floors, doors and window-sashes. In the recesses of the windows are broad seats. Within the memory of some of the residents of the town the panes of glass were of diamond shape. The height of the first story is 7⅔ feet; the height of the second is 6¾ feet. At the southerly corner in the second story there was originally an embrasure about a foot wide with a stone flooring, which remains. The exterior walls are now closed up, but not the walls within. The walls of the front and back of the house terminate at the floors of the attic, and the rafters lie upon them. The angle of the roof is sixty degrees, making the base and sides equal. At the end of the wing, by the chimney, is a recess which must have been intended as a place of concealment. The interior wall has the appearance of touching the chimney like the wall at the northwest end, but the removal of a board discovers two closets, which project beyond the lower part of the building."

Writing about the house Mrs. Cone, the present owner, says: It was built as a place of refuge from the Indians, also as a place of public worship. The partitions in the main building were movable and folded up like a fan and were fastened to the rafters by what they called keys, iron staples with a crossbar that turned in a socket. When fastened up the whole house was one room. There was no second floor. The east wing was a still smaller building with only two rooms and some small closets. There were chimneys on the south and east sides like the one now standing on the north. The one on the south was taken down before Jasper Griffing bought the house in 1776, why, I do not know, but the wall was weakened by the process, and two iron bars were put in to strengthen it, and are still to be seen on the outside, unless covered with vines. When the repairs were made in 1868 all the woodwork of the rear building was saved. It was oak and probably cut in 1639. Some of it was used for the banister and newel of the present stairs, which are very poor specimens of work, as the oak was so hard that modern tools could not take hold of it. I have some chairs made of it."

A year or two ago [c1896] the Daughters of the American Revolution placed a tablet inscribed with the appropriate historical note in the face of the building.

THE SPENCER–PIERCE HOUSE [GARRISON HOUSE], NEWBURYPORT, MASSACHUSETTS

"There is considerable doubt and uncertainty in regard to the date when this ancient stone house was built. Some authorities claim that it was erected by John Spencer between the years 1635 and 1637, and others assert that it was built for his nephew, John Spencer, Jr., between 1640 and 1650; and still others are of the opinion that its first owner and occupant was Daniel Pierce, who bought the farm in 1651. Careful examination of the records at Salem, made with special reference to the preparation of this sketch, does not furnish sufficient evidence to determine the question beyond a reasonable doubt; but it has led to the discovery of some important facts, now for the first time published, that may be of assistance in arriving at the correct conclusion. It would be impossible to give in detail all the deeds, wills, and other legal instruments that have been consulted, without extending this sketch beyond its proper limits; and therefore only a brief outline of these papers will be inserted here, with such quotations and comments as will enable the reader to follow the changes that have taken place in the ownership of this property from 1635 to the present time.

"When the age of this old house, with its picturesque exterior, the solid masonry of its walls, and the men who have owned and occupied it, is considered and allowed to quicken the thought and imagination, it tells an interesting story of old Colonial days. There are few residences in New England that are more attractive or fascinating. Its style of architecture is remarkable, considering the early date at which it was built. Its walls are composed of several varieties of stone; and some of them must have been brought from a long distance, perhaps by means of boats or rafts down the Merrimack River. The bricks used in the construction of the front porch, as well as the square tile which form the floor, were probably brought from England. Brickyards were established at Salem and Medford previous to 1680; but the finished product of those yards was of an inferior quality, and the size of the bricks was fixed by order of the General Court, as follows: 'Every brick shall measure 9 inches long, 2½ inches thick, and 4½ inches wide.' Imported English brick were much smaller and more smoothly moulded.

"The house was built in the form of a cross. On the northern projection, where the kitchen is located, a tall brick chimney rises from a stone foundation, outside the rear wall.

"'The great porch of this old house,' writes Mrs. Harriet Prescott Spofford, in an article published in *Harper's Magazine* for July, 1875, 'is said to be the most beautiful architectural specimen in this part of the country, although it doubtless owes part of its beauty to the mellow and varied coloring which two hundred years have given it. Yet the bevelled bricks of its arches and casements and the exquisite nicety of its ornamentation lead the careful scrutinizer to side with those who dismiss the idea of its having been a garrison house and to conjecture that that idea gained currency from the fact that it was once used to store powder in—a fact that was fixed in the popular memory by an explosion there which blew out the side of the house, and landed an old slave of the occupant on her bed in the boughs of an adjacent apple-tree.'"—From *Ould Newbury*, by John J. Currier. Boston: Damrell & Upham. 1896.

THE CRADOCK HOUSE, MEDFORD, MASSACHUSETTS

"In the *Historical Register* for October, 1898, published by the Medford Historical Society, are articles by William Cushing Wait and Walter H. Cushing, which go to disprove the argument that the present building is the original homestead. Both place the original Cradock House on the spot where the Garrison House stands, back of the Medford Savings Bank. The present 'Garrison House' has always been known by that name.

"The principal evidence is comprised in two early maps. The first was found among the Sloane manuscripts in the British Museum. It is believed to have been published about 1633, and has marginal notes in Governor Winthrop's hand.

"'The most important part of the map to us in Medford,' says Mr. Wait, 'is the house sketched near the ford, and the word 'Meadford,' with Governor Winthrop's reference to it: Meadford: Mr. Cradock ferme (farm) house.' No house is indicated near the location of the building we have so long boasted as the Cradock House, built in 1634. It is true this map is earlier than 1634, but if Governor Cradock's farmhouse was near the ford in 1633 it is probable no change was made the next year.'

"The other map is one made by Governor Winthrop in 1637, of his farm at Ten Hills, now a part of Somerville. This shows the same group of buildings near the ford as the other map.

"In an article on 'Governor Cradock's Plantation,' Walter H. Cushing says: —

"'From an affidavit in the Middlesex County Court, in the case of Gleison *vs.* Davidson *et al.*, it would appear that Davison had also preceded Mayhewes, for Joseph Hill testifies 'that about 1633 Mr. Nic Davison lived at Meadford House and that Mr. Mayhew did not then dwell at Meadford House.' This affidavit is also interesting as showing that in 1633 there was a certain building of sufficient prominence to be designated as 'Meadford House.'

"The location of that house, or of the Cradock House, if they are identical, is not absolutely known. Tradition has, during the last two or three generations, pointed to the old brick building on Riverside Avenue. But tradition is notoriously a bad guide, and, unsupported by evidence, is as often wrong as right. Facing page 120 of this number of the *Register* is a reproduction of a map of Governor Winthrop's, supposed by critics to have been made about 1634. The place marked 'Mr. Cradock's farme house,' does not correspond, even making due allowance for inaccuracies, to the neighborhood of the Riverside Avenue house, but is considerably farther up the river, as can be seen by referring to the road from Salem to the ford at the Mystic. Moreover, it is at the head of navigation of the river. Far more definite, however, than this map is that of Winthrop's farm at Ten Hills. Medford is shown as a group of buildings situated near the northern end of the bridge. No other buildings are given, and the half-dozen on the map apparently belong to one estate. Now, in 1637, Medford and Governor Cradock's farm were identical. Furthermore, as Winthrop and Cradock were close friends, such a prominent building as the latter's house would not be omitted, if

any buildings were given. Here, then, it seems to me, is almost conclusive evidence of the location of the house near the square. So much from the maps.

"'In his will Cradock does not specify the number or location of the buildings bequeathed; neither do the heirs when they convey to Edward Collins. But when the latter, in 1661, sells 1,600 acres of the farm to Richard Russell, the limit on the east is set by the old Nowell and Wilson (then Blanchard) farms, while the western boundary is a brook west of the Mansion House. This brook ran out of a swamp near the northern line between Charlestown and the farm, and, according to the dimensions and known boundaries of the conveyance, must have been Meeting House Brook. When Russell, in 1669, sells Jonathan Wade three-quarters of this tract he reserves the fourth, lying next to the Blanchard farm (*i. e.,* Wellington) and farthest from the dwelling-house. When Jonathan Wade died, in 1689, the inventory of his property included a brick house near the bridge; and that house is still standing, north of the savings-bank. Now, it does not at all follow that these three buildings are identical, but it is certain that the principal house, the dwelling or mansion house of this estate, from the time of Collins to Wade, was in the neighborhood of Medford Square.'

"To sum up: 1. No evidence has been brought to light for the house on Riverside Avenue. 2. What evidence there is points to a house near the square. 3. The Ten Hills farm map suggests strongly the site of the present Garrison House, if not the house itself.'"

THE LEFFERTS HOMESTEAD, FLATBUSH AVENUE, BROOKLYN, NEW YORK

The present owner of this house, Mr. John Lefferts, Jr., writes: "The old house on Flatbush Avenue in this city has been in the occupancy of the Lefferts family for many years. We have no definite data of the age of this house. It has always been owned and occupied by a member of the Lefferts family, and handed down from one generation to another. My father, the late Mr. John Lefferts of Flatbush, always supposed that the house was built about 1750; at any rate, it stood there for several years previous to the Revolutionary War, for during and before the Battle of Long Island it was occupied by a Lefferts. About forty years ago, my father built an addition in the rear of this house, of a type of architecture entirely foreign to the old structure. He has often told me he regretted this, for it spoils, to some extent, the beauty of the old house when looking at it from its side. It was done, however, when there was not much attention paid to architectural effect in this part of the country. I am not an

Doorway
LEFFERTS HOMESTEAD — c1750 — 563 FLATBUSH
AVENUE, BROOKLYN, NEW YORK

INDEPENDENCE HALL — 1729–1734 —
PHILADELPHIA, PENNSYLVANIA

After the restoration

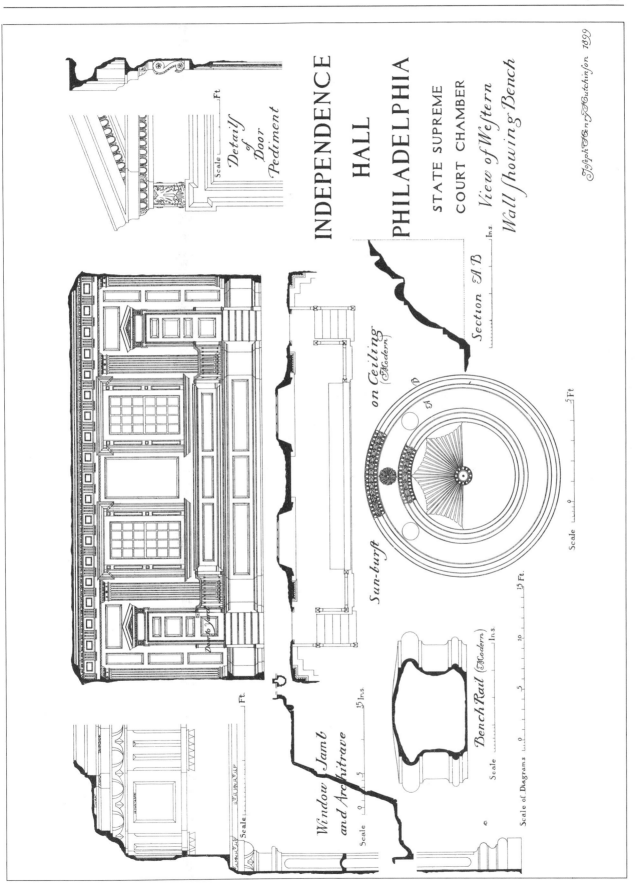

Detail
of
Door
Pediment

Scale ⌐____⌐ Ft

INDEPENDENCE
HALL
PHILADELPHIA

STATE SUPREME
COURT CHAMBER
*View of Weſtern
Wall ſhowing Bench*

Section A B

⌐____⌐ Ins.

Joſeph Henry Hutchinſon 1899

Sun-burſt on Ceiling
(Modern)

Scale ⌐____⌐ 5 Ft

Door to Yard

Window Jamb
and Architrave

Scale ⌐____⌐ 15 Ins.

Scale ⌐____⌐ Ft.

Bench Rail (Modern)

Scale ⌐____⌐ Ins.

Scale of Diagrams ⌐____⌐ 15 Ft.

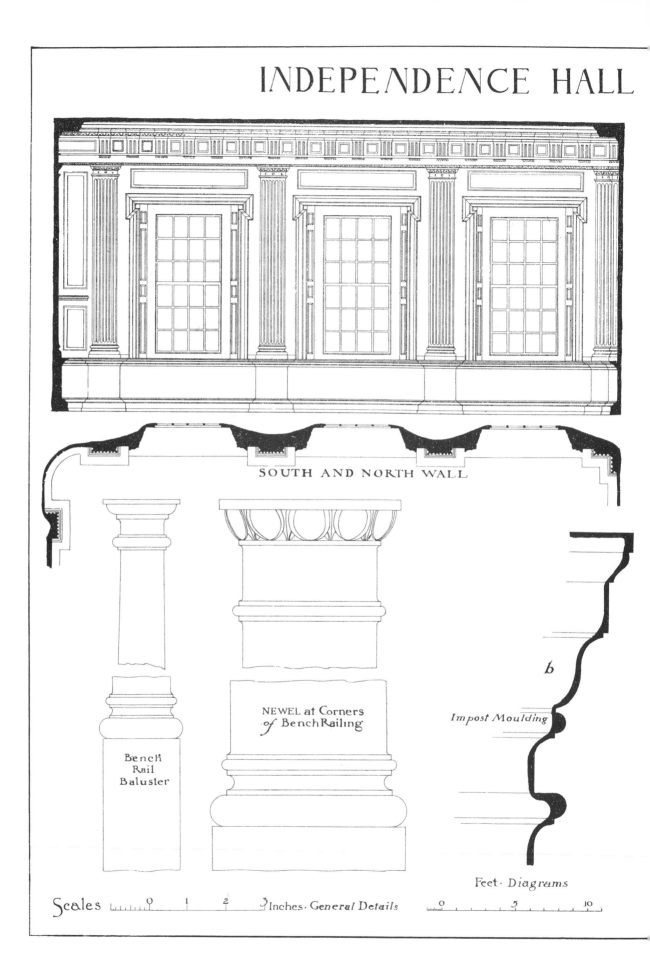

SOUTH AND NORTH WALL

Bench
Rail
Baluster

NEWEL at Corners
of Bench Railing

Impost Moulding

b

Feet · Diagrams

Scales · · · 0 · 1 · 2 · 3 Inches · *General Details* · 0 · 5 · 10

PHILADELPHIA

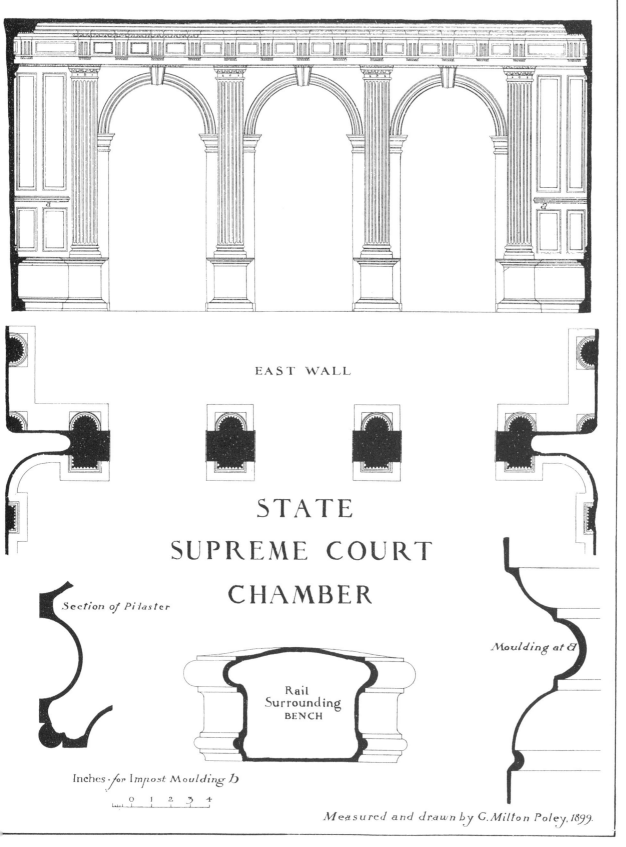

EAST WALL

STATE
SUPREME COURT
CHAMBER

Section of Pilaster

Moulding at d

Rail
Surrounding
BENCH

Inches · *for Impost Moulding* ♭

0 1 2 3 4

Measured and drawn by G. Milton Poley, 1899.

TAYLOR HOUSE — c1790 — ROXBURY, MASSACHUSETTS

Dutch and German
Eighteenth-Century Work

Text by
Unknown Author
Originally published in 1902 as
Volume III of The Georgian Period

ST. GEORGE'S CHURCH — 1800 —
HALIFAX, NOVA SCOTIA

DUTCH AND GERMAN
EIGHTEENTH-CENTURY WORK

PROBABLY more than one person while looking over the chapters on British architecture in Volume XV, has wondered how it happened that during his travels in Great Britain he never noticed how large was the number, and how varied the interest, of the buildings that, seemingly, exist on every hand designed in the style with which this work especially concerns itself. These Colonial doorways are so familiarly agreeable at home in America, how was it, then, that their presence in England escaped notice? How was it that houses sided with clapboards, looking as if they had overnight crossed over from Salem, were passed by without detection? We never suspected such structures were to be found outside of this country, yet Mr. Davie and his camera have found them, and when they are brought before the reader on the book page he at once recognizes that here is something novel, a fresh fact that had escaped his traveler's notebook; that here at last is the germ of the familiar wooden house of his native land, the home of his forefathers, who carried the memory of it with them in their exile, and erected modified simulacra of it at the earliest convenient opportunity.

The explanation is simple. The traveler voyages in search of novelties, new impressions; he seeks new ideas which, perhaps, he can transplant, graft, prune, cross and improve in divers ways. The female eye is caught by, and retains the memory of, unusual fashions of dressing the hair, new shapes of caps, unusual combinations of colors, while the male mind retains memories of the ridiculously heavy harnesses, the solid and unwieldly vehicles, the unhandy-looking tools, and so on. Of a Fifth Avenue belle and a Breton fisherwoman seen side by side on the same beach in Brittany, the woman traveler would see and retain the memory of the latter only, just as the man, though he had passed an American buggy and an English tax-cart side by side on the road to the Derby, would warmly declare, after reaching home, that he had seen no American "rig" anywhere abroad. In the same way, the architectural traveler would recall the strange appearance of the housefronts on the Continent, with their great unfinished holes where the casement windows had swung open inwards, and would declare that nowhere did he see a hung sash or guillotine window. Familiarity breeds contempt, and things contemptible or too familiar generally escape notice, so it is not to be wondered that the homelike structures of the Georgian period have not attracted the notice of American travelers, except perhaps in the matter of Wren's churches: they have unquestionably been noted and, in cases, deservedly admired. But Wren's churches, like Michaelangelo's dome, or Raphael's Madonnas, are amongst the literary puppets that every writer is expected to parade upon his stage at the auspicious moment, and, consequently, few readers can escape knowledge of them.

Presently, for the American traveler, much of the quondam pleasure of the Continental tour will be lost through the process of vulgarizing that is going on so fast. The glory of the châteaux in the valley of the Loire will wane, since what novelty will they possess for the traveler who winters in North Carolina, summers in Newport, spends the autumn at Lenox, and so has become familiar with French châteaux — as bettered by the American designer? Better he knows they are, since they have electric elevators, steam heat, refrigerating plants and other appliances of high-pressure

GOVERNMENT HOUSE — 1801–1805 —
HALIFAX, NOVA SCOTIA

American civilization, and so not to be placed in the same category with those homes of the old French aristocrat, with their draughty rooms and their cold and noisy wooden floors. And the traveler familiar with New York will feel no thrill before the lordly palaces of Genoa and Rome, for has he not seen such as they from his childhood up? Even the seemingly inimitable flavor of Venice is likely not to be savored by the American, by and by, who has acquired the "exposition-habit," and has become accustomed, once a year at least, to loll at his ease in the smooth-going gondola. The thought is more piteous than exasperating, but the outcome seems inevitable, and the traveler of the future is likely to follow the prescribed route in a more discontented frame of mind than now. But now, as then, the traveler does not note the presence of familiar aspects and facts, and so it is small wonder that the illustrations in Volume XV present themselves somewhat in the light of a revelation.

It is rather a reversal of probabilities that a colonizing nation, whose youth are prone to leave home at the earliest opportunity and seek excitement and personal discomfort in every quarter of the globe, should be the nation of all others which understands how to make the dwelling places of its members look homelike, peaceful and comfortable. The French family feeling is much stronger than that of the English, but none would suspect it when he contrasts the tawdry eccentricities of the châteaux and *maisons de campagne* of the well-to-do upper-middle-class Frenchman with the plain and simple country-house of an Englishman of the same means and rank.

But, wanderer as he is by nature, the Englishman carries with him his home habits, and he is as unwilling to house himself in the building of the country he favors with his presence as he is unable to believe he can be personally clean unless he carries with his luggage a tin bathtub of unmistakable British make. The cities of India and the open ports of the East are sprinkled with buildings of recent date, all conceived in one phase or another of Victorian Gothic, while, on the other hand, the towns colonized by the French show how the more artistic people have been quick to seize on and adapt the methods, materials and designs native of the soil. It is a happy chance that the English colonists who settled in this country brought with them memories of Georgian and pre-Georgian buildings, and did not leave home in the time of a Gothic Revival; else, in place of our graceful Colonial mantelpieces, with their ample and useful mantelshelves, we might have found in our older dwellings fireplaces as cheerless and useless for home purposes as those which

OLD DUTCH CHURCH—1755—HALIFAX,
NOVA SCOTIA

Viollet-le-Duc has introduced in his restoration at Pierrefonds.

Wherever along our Eastern coast the Englishmen settled, we find, still, abundant traces of his presence in the houses and churches he erected. Not only are they to be found, as every one knows, widely scattered in the original thirteen states, but there are quite as interesting examples to be found in the British provinces to the north of us. French city as Quebec is, there is there to be found many an interesting example of Georgian architecture in whose conception and execution certainly no Frenchman had a share, and so it is with other places all the way from Halifax to Toronto. At the latter place the writer heard there was an old mansion of much interest in the Georgian style, and so addressed the present occupant for particulars and permission to procure the desired photographs. In reply came a chilling, and quite Britannic, response which declared that it was quite unnecessary to take any trouble in the matter, as the structure was merely a simple English house of brick with a pillared porch or two. As the real point of interest lay in the fact that a "simple English house" should have been built of brick as far west as that—quite on the outskirts of civilization—a hundred years ago, such a response coming from anyone would have been exasperating, but it was all the more so since the owner was a well-known man of letters who might have been expected to appreciate the purpose of the inquiry. Still, as the statement was made that the house had been altered within recent years, it did not seem worthwhile to press further an evidently unwilling householder. But there, beyond the source of the St. Lawrence, was built shortly after the Revolution, and possibly with imported brick, a "simple English house" in the Georgian style.

The earliest architectural efforts made by the first settlers in the British province were doubtless similar to those made in the more southerly settlements, save that the greater rigor of the climate demanded more substantial buildings; but by the end of the eighteenth century all, or nearly all, of the structures reared by the early settlers had probably passed away, and the architecture of the time was affected by the same influences that created the meeting house of New England and the mansion of the Virginia gentleman. But, though English influence in a seaport town was, of course, strong, and though Halifax was within the radius of the influence that radiated from the French settlements, there were other influences at work there, other bands of settlers had come from other lands than France and England and left traces of their presence, both in the admixture of blood and customs and in the buildings they erected, *more suo*. Thus, there are at Halifax two very interesting ecclesiastical structures, one of which avowedly, and the other inferentially, bears testimony to the early date at which the common people of this northern continent began to be evolved by a species of ethnical cross-breeding which has no parallel in the world's history. Even the great Roman Empire only succeeded in producing a sort of effeminate hybrid, a human mule, unable to perpetuate its own species.

Here at Halifax is a little Dutch church built in 1755, about as simple a little structure as could well be devised; its parts so simple and so obviously arranged that it would seem quite unlikely that they could tell much of an architectural story or say with much distinctness that the structure was devised by other than English minds. Yet, the low wall, the wide roof, the door and window heads hard against the wall-plate, the door at one end of the long side, not in the middle of the gable end, and, above all, the spire on the low tower, with its almost flat broaches, tell the observer unmistakably that the building is of German or Dutch derivation. And so it is, but whether the one or the other, whether built by some streamlet from the great German immigration that had accidentally been deflected northward from its true course, or whether some band of real Dutchmen, trying to return home after the English had dislodged them from New Amsterdam, had been disheartened, or, being windbound by adverse winds, had put in to what was to be Halifax, and, being satisfied, had there remained, is not material. The really interesting fact is that at the very same time that buildings designed in the Georgian style were being erected in different parts of America there were being built in different places by immigrants of Teutonic stock, or those immigrants' descendants, other structures that distinctly recall the elements of the architecture of their fatherland as they best could remember and interpret them.

This little church received a government grant, probably quite as minute as its own size, the rest of the

ST. PAUL'S CHURCH — c1750 — HALIFAX,
NOVA SCOTIA

building fund being contributed by members of the congregation who worshipped here, after the tenets of the Lutheran Church, until circumstances led to amalgamation of this society and another. Since that time the building has been in use as a school, no great change of course, for, in all probability, the early churches or meeting houses were in most cases used as schoolhouses on workdays.

The society which received the adhesion of the members of the old Dutch Lutheran Church is, curiously enough, one which has always abided by the prescriptions of the thirty-nine articles of the Established Church of England, and this may be taken as showing how the pietistic fervor of the Lutheran fathers had, in a couple of generations, become ameliorated in their grandsons. Architecturally speaking, there is no other church in Halifax to which the owners of the Old Dutch Church could, with so much propriety, have migrated as to St. George's, a church of a very unusual type, a distinctly un-English type, a North German or, more nearly, a Scandinavian type, and it may be a freak of real atavism that drew the migrating Lutherans to this curious and interesting structure. But the warmest supporters of the claims of Leif Ericson would hardly dare to found an argument in favor of the Scandinavian as the original discoverer of this continent on the architectural character of St. George's, for the structure itself was built as late as 1800, and if it replaced an earlier structure, on a larger scale while maintaining its essential features, we do not know that it is so.

St. Paul's Church, a very large structure, since it will hold a congregation of two thousand persons, is, so far as the actual beginning of its being is concerned, really an older structure than St. George's or the Old Dutch Church, and, as it was begun only a year or two after the arrival of Governor Cornwallis with his original

band of settlers actually in 1750 — about the time the beautiful tower and spire of the church at Farmington, Connecticut, was finished — one might hope to find some evidence of kinship between it and some of the more interesting of the New England meeting houses, all the more from the fact that St. Paul's was framed in Boston. Perhaps Boston, having in this way aided in promoting godliness amongst the progenitors of the "blue noses," found there was nothing particularly ungodly in appropriating, without payment, at a later day the timbers out of which were worked the columns of the portico of the Massachusetts State House. But, as the illustration shows, St. Paul's was built rather to accommodate the troops in garrison than to give expression to architectural beauty, and its tower, while individual enough, is neither graceful nor interesting. Moreover, the entire exterior of the building was palpably restored at the time the low side aisles were added, not many years ago. In the same way, the tower of the Old Town Clock, as it is called, which dates from about the same time, has none of the refinement of the best New England work of the time, and, as it too has been "restored," it is questionable whether the circular peristyle is or is not part of the original design.

All of the buildings thus far mentioned are of wood, but wood used in a rather commonplace way, and handled evidently by workmen who had not access to any of the Builder's Assistants which unquestionably enabled the mechanics of New England to turn out work of greater delicacy, interest and refinement than did the mechanics to the south or to the north of them. In stone, however, the builders succeeded better in giving to their work the architectural character of the period, and in Halifax there are two or three interesting buildings: one, the Admiralty House, a simple but dignified square structure with low-pitched hip roof, is evidently later in date than the others, which, like it, are public structures, and so had the benefit of the best architectural talent. Of these two, the Government House, the official residence of the Lieutenant-Governor, is an extremely well-proportioned building characterized by slightly projecting flanking pavilions which recall the arrangement of the typical houses of colonial Virginia and, further, are characterized by "swell fronts" upon each pavilion, quite after the Boston manner. In fact, the official residences of the time are particularly happy in their architectural effect, if it is fair to base such an opinion upon this building and the almost equally interesting Government House at Fredericton, New Brunswick. The Halifax building was erected in the years 1801–1805. The other Halifax building, even more admirable, is the Province Building, which was erected

OLD TOWN CLOCK, HALIFAX, NOVA SCOTIA

in 1811–1819 at a cost of a little over two hundred thousand dollars.

The one building in Halifax, however, of strikingly foreign aspect is unquestionably the Old Dutch Church, and in this case we do not feel called on to question the propriety of the attribution. But as much cannot be said for the many other "Dutch" structures that can be found in various parts of the country, for, in many a case, the term must be translated as one today translates the term "Pennsylvania Dutch," and remember that it more often means German, or even Swedish, than Netherlandish. We have been greatly disappointed at not being able to produce any tangible evidence of the influence the Dutch fashions of building had upon the work of the Georgian designers and builders in this country, and we are inclined to feel that such influence as was exerted was not direct, but sifted first through England. The indefinable Dutch feeling that can be perceived in some of the towers and spires of the New England meeting houses evidently has no distinct prototype in Holland, but is unquestionably based upon Wren's working out of his impressions of his own travels in Holland. In like manner, when in some of the small brick churches and court houses in the South one feels that at last he has found unmistakably the connecting link, it is pretty

certain that the next turning over of the records of English work of the time will bring to light some market house or petty assize-court, which, though Dutch in feeling, is much more likely to be the real prototype of the American example. There is many a village street in England fronted with low brick buildings which gives the traveler the momentary impression that he is back again in Holland, but when he looks about and strives to localize the impression it eludes him. He feels sure the impression must have its justification, but how or with what he can support it, he finds it impossible to say. So we are inclined to think that, aside from the immediate neighborhood of New York, the work of the Hollander had little direct influence on the building done in this country during the eighteenth century, and this is all the more disappointing since one of the myths relating to the gambrel roof is that is was derived from Holland. Perhaps it was, but we hope it was not; for if there is any feature that is distinctive of American work it is the gambrel roof, and one would like to feel that it was evolved in this country out of the sheer constructive necessities of the early builders.

If the changes of more than two centuries have left on and near Manhattan Island, where alone it could properly be sought for, few traces of real Dutch work,

OLD GOVERNMENT HOUSE — 1828 —
FREDERICTON, NEW BRUNSWICK

it is far otherwise with the "Dutch" work that is properly to be credited to the Teuton of northern and southern Germany, and as streamlets of the great German immigration filtered to all parts of the Atlantic seaboard from Maine to Georgia, evidences of the half-remembered architectural fashions of the German fatherland are to be found to this day in many widely scattered places. But as it was William Penn who was largely responsible for this remarkable immigration, first through his exhortations to the sectaries when as a young man he wandered through Germany, and later, after he became a "proprietor," through the pamphlets, descriptive of the province of Pennsylvania and how there was to be found there freedom from war, religious persecution and the oppressiveness of unjust laws, which in French, Dutch, English and German he sent broadcast through Europe, it was natural that the largest number of these immigrants should settle in Pennsylvania. It is not our part to explain how and why these immigrants, wearied with the constant bloodshed of the War of the Spanish Succession, and still more wearied by the poverty forced upon them because of it, and subjected to heavy taxation everywhere, while in some states under Catholic rule the believers in the new creeds — and there were many varieties — were oppressed and persecuted to an unendurable degree, were ready to abandon their homes and risk the perils of a long journey to an unknown and undeveloped country. Nor is it our part to dilate on the dismal tale of their journeyings: how many fell by the way in their tramp across Europe; how more were unable to get farther than England, and there remained to the number of thousands, a charge upon the government and charitable private individuals; how those who crossed the sea endured in the small vessels of the day, ill-found and half-provisioned,

treatment from brutal shipmasters that puts tales of the "middle passage" to shame — on one ship sailing in 1732 with 150 passengers 100 of them died during the passage, and in 1758, out of the passengers carried during that year in fifteen ships 2,000 died, while in another ship that carried 312 passengers 250 died during the voyage. But this terrible mortality prevailed mainly in the time when the "Newlanders" had built up their nefarious traffic, which resulted essentially in landing the immigrants — such as survived — in this country as actual slaves to those who paid their passage money, whether before they started or after they arrived. Immigrants thus enslaved or mortgaged became known as Redemptioners, and they were held in bondage under the formal precepts of enacted law until by their labor they could pay off their debts, and their masters took uncommon care that this task should be made none too easy for them.

The movement — a very large and long-continued one — is one of the extremely interesting events in our early history, and because of the wide distribution of the arrivals, partly by accident and partly by design — Penn was not the only landowner to profit by this German aspiration for a free and peaceful life — it made a vast impression on the country, and has left traces in many places besides Pennsylvania, traces which consist largely in place names and family names, in a diluted strain of German blood and temperament and something in the way of buildings. No trace now remains of the Labadist settlement at Bohemia Manor in Maryland, on the Chesapeake, and the same, we believe, can be said of the Lutheran settlement at Waldoboro, Maine; but the settlement at Quincy, Massachusetts, has at least left a name, for that part of the town where the Sailors' Snug Harbor lies is still styled Germantown. Charleston and Savannah were the recipients of many Germans, but their chief foothold in South Carolina was at Ebenezer, Orangeburg, and Saxe-Gotha. In Virginia, Winches-

PROVINCE BUILDING — 1811–1819 —
HALIFAX, NOVA SCOTIA

MORAVIAN BUILDINGS, BETHLEHEM,
PENNSYLVANIA
This drawing, combined from three different
photographs, is faulty in perspective.

ter, Shepherdstown, Strasburg and Woodstock are likely to afford evidence of the presence of early German inhabitants, and there were many settlements made in North Carolina by Germans who did not find in Pennsylvania the opportunities they sought.

It is in Pennsylvania, however, that is to be found more evidence of the German immigration than elsewhere, and as the first settlement was made at Germantown, that suburb of Philadelphia is still rich in a kind of derived German feeling. How many buildings there still are positively erected by the German immigrants we will not attempt to say, but as the great German movement—although Pastorius bought his land in Germantown in 1683—did not begin till 1709, and reached its flood only in 1738, while the high-tide mark of the Redemptionist movement was not reached till 1753, it is plainly possible that there should be many buildings still standing in Pennsylvania that owe their being to the hands of actual German immigrants and not to their descendants of the next generation. In Philadelphia itself one should not expect to find much work of German feeling, for Philadelphia was the home of Quakers, men of peace, men, moreover, of considerable wordly wisdom, and they brought it about that as fast as the Germans arrived they should be forwarded to the interior and made to found settlements along the frontier, where, as many of them had borne arms at home, their knowledge of military affairs and willingness to defend their heads with their hands made them an admirable vanguard of civilization, and at the same time a safeguard for the peaceable Quakers in Philadelphia. And right valiantly did these German frontiersmen play their part, not only in Indian warfare and at the siege of Quebec, but in the Revolution. So it is that one must seek in Lancaster,

Ephrata, Bethlehem, Lititz, Easton, Allentown, Reading and the country between for early indications of German occupation. But the Germans were so many—Franklin estimating their number at three-fifths of the entire population of the state and other authorities declaring a higher ratio—and so widely scattered that not only are there many buildings of unquestionable German origin still standing all over the state, but they have had such an influence on the commonly adopted style of building that Pennsylvania buildings have an air of their own, quite different from that to be found in other states—plain, substantial, broad and big-roofed, and more often of stone than of brick, the stonework as often stuccoed as not.

As the German immigration was largely a movement of the sectaries who held varied forms of belief and followed different practices, it was natural that each sect should establish an independent settlement, some so small that they quickly passed out of exis-

GEMEINHAUS—1742—BETHLEHEM,
PENNSYLVANIA

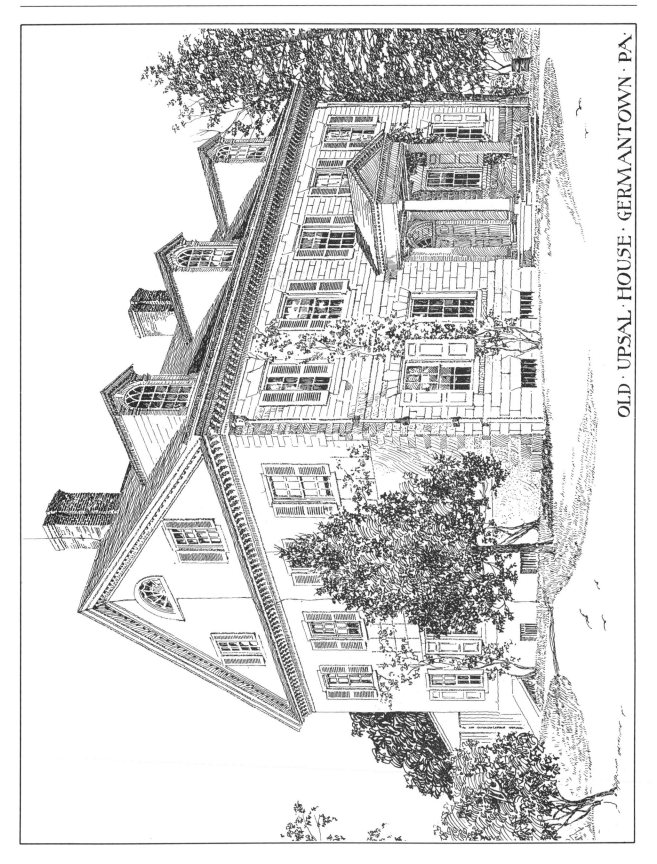

OLD · UPSAL · HOUSE · GERMANTOWN · PA·

·THE · OLD · CHEW · HOUSE · GERMANTOWN · PA·

Detail of Mantel
UPSAL MANSION, GERMANTOWN,
PENNSYLVANIA

Detail of Mantel
UPSAL MANSION, GERMANTOWN,
PENNSYLVANIA

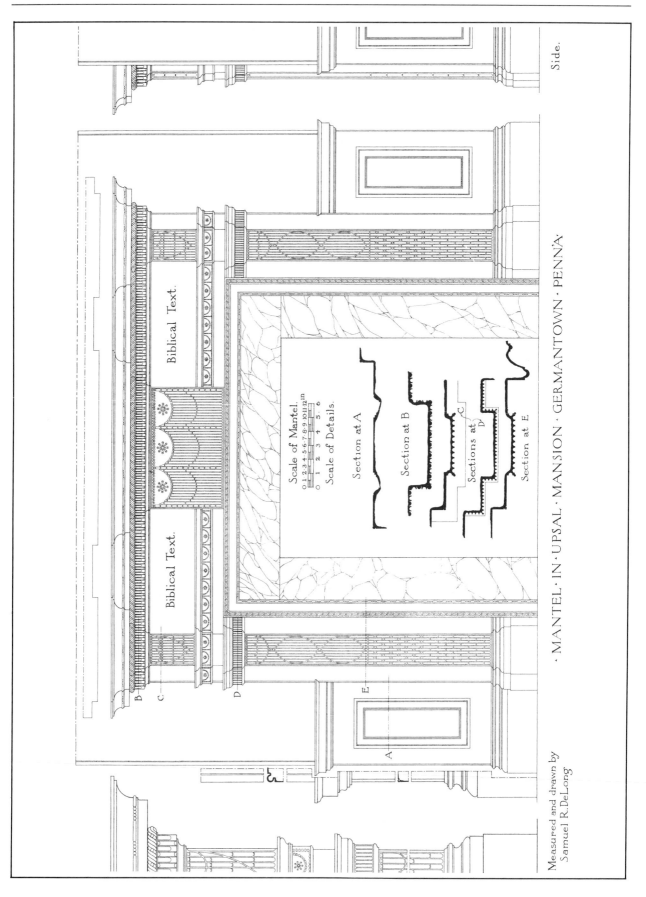

Side.

Biblical Text.

Biblical Text.

Scale of Mantel.
0 1 2 3 4 5 6 7 8 9 10 11 12 ^{in}

Scale of Details.
0   1   2   3   4   5   6

Section at A

Section at B

Sections at D C

Section at E

· MANTEL · IN · UPSAL · MANSION · GERMANTOWN · PENN'A·

Measured and drawn by
Samuel R. DeLong

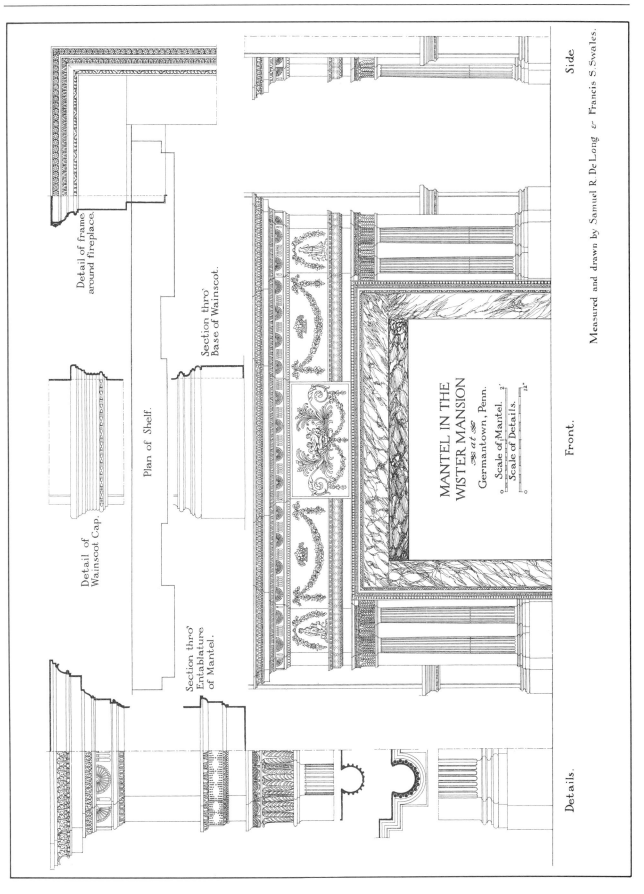

Detail of frame around fireplace.

Section thro' Base of Wainscot.

Plan of Shelf.

Detail of Wainscot Cap.

Section thro' Entablature of Mantel.

MANTEL IN THE WISTER MANSION
ఞ at ఞ
Germantown, Penn.

Scale of Mantel.
Scale of Details.

Front.

Side.

Measured and drawn by Samuel R. De Long & Francis S. Swales.

Details.

MORAVIAN CHURCH—1803—BETHLEHEM,
PENNSYLVANIA

tence, while others lingered longer, until the following generations, unable to stand the pressure of modern civilization, abandoned the seclusion of their fathers, foreswore their beliefs in a measure, and became everyday American citizens. And so, one after another, many of the different communal settlements changed their character, and the communal buildings were devoted to alien uses; but some still exist, as at Ephrata, which are measurably devoted to their original purposes; while other communities, as Bethlehem for instance, have known how to retain in a considerable degree traditions and practices, and at the same time to so modify and adapt them to the ideas of the time as to make their inherited practices a sort of drawing card to attract at certain seasons a considerable concourse of strangers, whose coming is a material help to the town.

The choral festival at Bethlehem is a musical performance of the first rank, but though its roots run far back, and though its renderings are not light-minded at all, yet the choruses are drilled by hired choirmasters, as any mere secular and moneymaking choir might be. The Bach festival last year was a very notable performance, and was but the latest overt manifestation of that love of music which the original settlers brought with them, which has persisted in varying forms until now, but always as a notable characteristic of the people and the place. One of these manifestations is found in the playing of trombones—and it is said that skillful players make trombones very effective musical instruments. In some New England churches, and possibly in more English churches, the bass-viol is still used in lieu of the organ to give a background for

choral or congregational singing, and travelers know how in some foreign churches trumpets, bugles and trombones are used for the same purpose. But at Bethlehem the trombone is *par excellence* the instrument, and its use, or rather one of its uses, has had a curious effect on architecture. Just as in some towns the "passing-bell" is tolled in the church tower as the weary soul has just taken its flight, the same function is at Bethlehem discharged by official trombone players, four in number, whose duty it is to ascend to the tower of the church and there blow to the four quarters of the town the news that brother or sister, maid, man or widow lies a-dying, the age, sex and marital condition of the departing being indicated by the choral that is played. This custom brings it about that the church tower must be provided with a platform or gallery, around which the players can pass, and from which they can blow their mournful messages.

The Moravians[1] of Bethlehem, while retaining their creed and racial relations, have advanced with the times and known how not to fall behind the chariot of progress, and so have been able to keep their buildings in good repair, and they form a very interesting group indeed: the big Moravian Church, built in 1803; the First Seminary, built in 1746, flanked on one side of the open court yard that fronts it by the Second Clergy House that was built four years earlier, and on the other side by the Sisters' House, built in the same year, are worth going some distance to see in this country because of their distinctly foreign flavor. The Old

OLD CHAPEL—1751—BETHLEHEM,
PENNSYLVANIA

[1] MORAVIAN SETTLEMENTS—Bethlehem was settled in 1741; Ephrata in 1743; Old Nazareth in 1743 (Nazareth Hall dates from 1755); Gnadenthal, 1745; Christian Spring, 1748; Friedensthal, 1750. The Barony of Nazareth was sold by the Penns to Edmuth Dorothea, Countess of Zinzendorf, who greatly assisted the emigrating Moravian sectaries.

Belfry
MORAVIAN CHURCH, BETHLEHEM,
PENNSYLVANIA

Chapel, with its big inclined buttresses, built in 1751, the Widow's House, built in 1768, and the Gemeinhaus, oldest of all, built in 1742, together with others belonging to the original community, form a curious contrast to the great industrial plant in the once quiet township which now turns out armor-plate and great guns.

The distinctively German origin of these buildings is found proved in the double ranges of dormers in the great roofs, and this German fashion of utilizing this roof space for dwelling purposes finds a curious echo, though a small one, in the headquarters of General Knox at Newburgh, New York, where in the print showing the rear view there can be seen, snuggled up against the chimneys, and running back to the house-ridge itself, two minute dormers. The Knox House is called Dutch, but these little dormers make us suspect that its Dutchiness has a Pennsylvania strain in it somewhere.

Very different in character indeed from the Moravian Church at Bethlehem is the Old Trappe Church at Collegeville, dedicated in 1745. This, the oldest Lutheran church in the country, was built, at a valuation of $1,000, for Henry Melchior Muhlenberg in 1743, and stands now practically as it was then. The structure is of stone stuccoed, and measures 39' x 54', and that the structure might not cost more than the sum appropriated even the women helped in the building of it. For one hundred and twenty-five years it was regularly used for Sunday and weekday services, but since the building of a larger church only one service each year is held in the building. It is unmistakably of a German type, and yet the gambrel roof, the general roof plan being also similar, recalls the Dutch church at Sleepy Hollow, in Tarrytown, New York, built so it is said, in 168–, and suggests the reflection that Americans, outside of Pennsylvania at least, have not had much use for German architecture. In the case of the Old Trappe, no one could for a moment question its foreign origin, its antiquity or its general interest, while the feeling that pervades the little church in Sleepy Hollow has been so imbibed and availed of by modern architects, there are so many thousand just such little country churches everywhere, that it is with difficulty one can bring oneself to believe in its real antiquity, its flavor is so very modern. The Sleepy Hollow Church, which is now used only in the summertime, and, in a sense, is under the guardianship of the Yonkers Historical and Library Association, was built soon after

GENERAL KNOX HEADQUARTERS,
NEWBURGH, NEW YORK

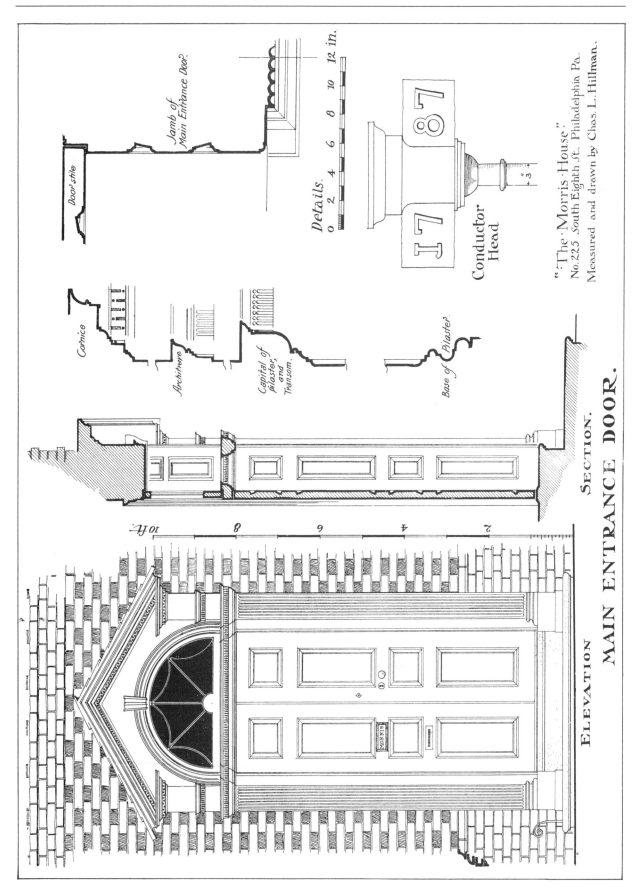

Jamb of Main Entrance Door.

Door.stile

Details.
0   2   4   6   8   10   12 in.

Conductor Head

1787

"The·Morris·House."
No. 225 South Eighth St. Philadelphia Pa.
Measured and drawn by Chas. L. Hillman.

Cornice

Architrave

Capital of pilaster, and Transom.

Base of Pilaster.

SECTION.

10 ft.
8
6
4
2

ELEVATION

MAIN ENTRANCE DOOR.

SLEEPY HOLLOW CHURCH — c1680 — TARRYTOWN, NEW YORK

OLD TRAPPE—1745—NEAR COLLEGEVILLE,
PENNSYLVANIA

accomplish his task in this very satisfactory manner. The interior is less changed than the exterior, and the general effect at least is the same that communicants in the early part of the eighteenth century had before them as they sat in the high-backed pews and lifted their chilled feet, now and then, from the brick-tiled floor, still in place. This church, the Gloria Dei in Philadelphia and one other[2] are amongst the rarities of our architectural treasures, and their quaintness is unquestionably due to their following types less familiar to us now than those derived from England, and simply go to impress once more on the observer what a very mixed origin the American people has.

Not far away, at New Castle, Delaware, is Immanuel Church, built in 1705, and an interesting type of the churches built by English congregations. It belongs to the same class as Christ Church at Williamsburg, Virginia, and Christ Church, Alexandria, and its tower, in comparison with the belfried towers of the Pennsylvania Dutch districts and the New England spired towers, as typified by Park Street Church, Boston, and Trinity Church, Newport, forms, as it were, a middle term between the two.

So many associations of a varied and always tender kind cluster about a church fabric that it is particularly easy to keep it in existence and, from the many interested, procure the needed money to keep it always in repair. Perhaps the most significant instance of this

1680 at the instigation of Katrina, second wife of Frederick Philipse, the first Lord of the Manor, or Patroon, of the Manor of Tarrytown.

Architecturally more interesting than either of these churches is Trinity, the Old Swedes Church at Wilmington, Delaware, built in 1698, and still in admirable repair and regular weekly use. We call it interesting, not only because it today offers a very picturesque effect, but because the several additions and restorations have been so well conceived and skillfully adjusted that few would imagine that the entire structure did not date from the same and a single epoch. Originally the church was a mere parallelogram, without tower, belfry or porch; still the easternmost and perhaps the other of the two transepts, or one-time porches, on the north side are believed to be nearly coeval with the body of the church. But the tower was added only in 1802; and at that time the canted hip roof at that end of the church which corresponded with that which still covers the eastern end of the church was happily done away with, and the gable simply butts against the tower in the most natural manner possible. Later, only some fifty years ago, the south porch, with its big round arch, was added, not for pride of architectural effect, but because it was found necessary to buttress the south wall, which was threatening to fall, and somene was artist enough to

OLD DOORWAY, ECONOMY, PENNSYLVANIA

[2] CHRIST (SWEDES) CHURCH, UPPER MERION TOWNSHIP—This building, the third of the early triad of united Swedish Lutheran churches, of which Gloria Dei, in Philadelphia, and the Old Swedes (Trinity) Church at Wilmington are the other two, was built in 1760. Up to 1831 the pastors were sent out from Sweden. The Episcopal ritual has been followed since that time.

WILLIAM PENN TAVERN, DELAWARE COUNTY,
PENNSYLVANIA

appreciation is the refusal within a year by the congregation of St. Paul's Church, Boston, to part with that building—not a very antiquated one—and its site for a million and a half of dollars, so that a great temple of trade might be built in its place. It is to be hoped, then, that just as these old church buildings are preserved and cherished with such tender solicitude by the descendants of the original congregations, and just as the various societies of Sons and Daughters of the Revolution and similar patriotic bodies are preserving, repairing and converting to museum purposes those semipublic buildings and houses which, like Stenton, the home of James Logan, in Philadelphia, have an historical and architectural worth, some similar organization will take it upon themselves to preserve the interesting buildings in Pennsylvania once occupied by communal sectaries of one kind or another. The Harmonists are in a flourishing condition, and so the interesting buildings at Economy, Pennsylvania, are likely to be properly cared for for a long time to come; but there are other places that are deserving of care, such as the buildings of the Monastic Society, or Seventh Day Baptist monks and nuns at Snow Hill, in Quincy Township, Pennsylvania, where, as the last member of the Society died in 1893, mere caretakers

now give to the monastery, mill and farm buildings a questionable amount of attention.

Perhaps other people do not share our idiosyncrasy, and so are perennially cognizant of the fact that North Carolina is one of the states of the Union, but we cannot help feeling that the state and the towns and villages therein are less known than any other part of this broad country. The German movement penetrated this region from Pennsylvania, and amongst other of the places settled by Germans at that time, Salem, settled by the Moravians in 1765, must be, if accounts are true, amongst the most interesting architecturally of the several settlements made by the sect. The church is said to be peculiarly interesting and quaint, partly because of the effect of the exceedingly small windows in the thick walls, high up, so that no Indian could shoot an arrow through some devotee as he listened to the weekly admonition of the pastor. There is evidently a good deal of "local color" at Salem which would make it worth one's while to attend the Easter festival there, share the "coffee and sweet buns," and listen to the melodious hymns, psalms and chorals with which the trombone players at the same time usher in the Easter sun and rouse the inhabitants from their slumbers for the annual celebration.

Interior
TRINITY (OLD SWEDES) CHURCH – 1698 –
WILMINGTON, DELAWARE

Interior
TRINITY (OLD SWEDES) CHURCH—1698—
WILMINGTON, DELAWARE

TRINITY (OLD SWEDES) CHURCH — 1698 —
WILMINGTON, DELAWARE

TRINITY (OLD SWEDES) CHURCH — 1698 —
WILMINGTON, DELAWARE

F

OLD COLONIAL HOVSE
NEAR CHAMOVNIX, FAIRMOVNT PARK,
PHILADELPHIA.

Scale
Details.

Measured by O.M.Hokanson
and Ira W.Hoover. O.M.H.Del.
1898.

Parlor Cornice

G

H

Interior Doors.

Door Architrave

Chair Rail.

Marble.

Section
thro'
A-B.

E

D

Details of Mantel.

Detail of And-iron.

A

E H F D

G

Grey Marble.

B

Plan of And-irons.

Brass.

PARLOR MANTEL.

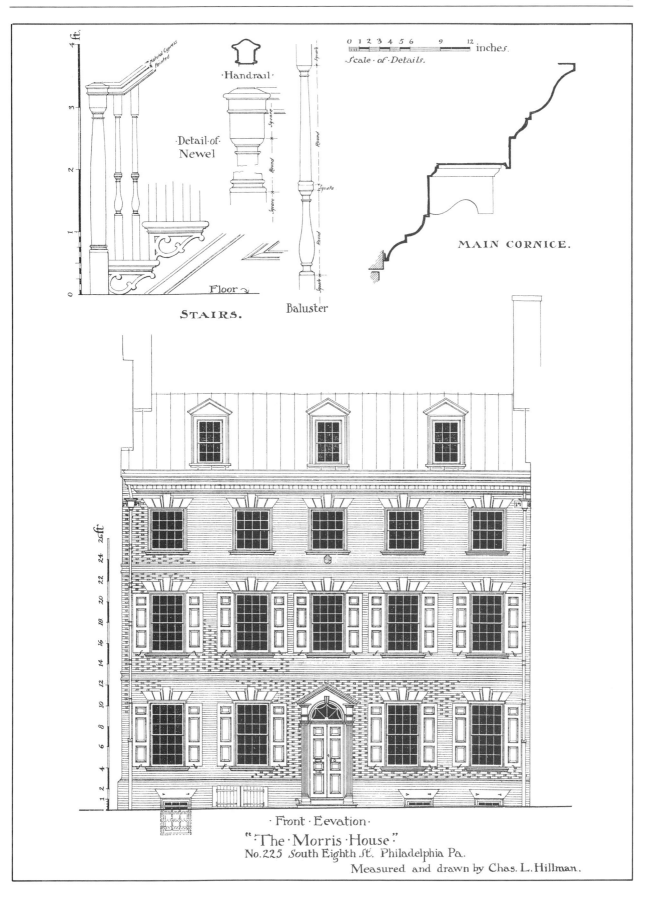

·Handrail·

·Detail·of·
Newel·

STAIRS.

Baluster

Floor

Scale·of·Details·

MAIN CORNICE.

· Front · Eevation ·
"·The·Morris·House·"
No. 225 South Eighth St. Philadelphia Pa.
Measured and drawn by Chas. L. Hillman.

RED LION TAVERN — 1730 — PHILADELPHIA
COUNTY, PENNSYLVANIA

But it is bootless and almost impossible to particularize the interesting buildings that grew from the German movement. Pennsylvania,[3] Virginia and North Carolina are old states, and it is a peculiarity of Pennsylvania that, whereas in other states frame buildings were normally used, here a great part of the buildings, of all kinds, were erected in stone, *au naturel*, or covered with stucco, as the case might be, and so, being substantial, have lasted practically unchanged to our day. So it is possible in Pennsylvania to find in many directions an abundance of structures erected in the early and middle part of the eighteenth century, though few would be discovered having any recognizable element of design that would lead one to class them with the "Old Colonial" buildings which chiefly concern us.

It is perhaps fortunate that Pennsylvania buildings are so generally built of stone, for it is evidently because of this that there has come down to us in good condition a very interesting relic of the great house, designed by L'Enfant, that Robert Morris, "the finan-

cier of the Revolution," partly completed on Chestnut Street, Philadelphia. Let into the face of the second-story wall of a little stone house in Conshohocken, just outside of Philadelphia, once occupied by James Traquier, a stone-cutter and one of the contractors for Morris's house, is a marble panel, sculptured in high relief by an Italian sculptor, Giuseppe Jardella, who had been imported to execute the carved work that was to adorn the great house. The panel which, by the courtesy of the publishers of *Monumental News*, we here illustrate, is dedicated to the fine arts, or to literature and painting, and taken with the pair of great marble Ionic capitals that stand in the yard behind the house — which adjoins the quarry from which the marble was taken — indicates how serious a loss it was to the architectural records of the country when disaster overtook the great financier, and his lordly house in its unfinished state was itself converted into a prison to relieve the overcrowded state of the jail in which its former owner was at that time lodged.

Men of business as well as men of peace, the Quakers of Philadelphia were the connecting link between the farmers and trappers of the interior and the mother country, and in prosecution of their business they and others had to travel widely over the state, and as Pennsylvania is not as well served with rivers as is

---

[3] OLD PAXTANG CHURCH, HARRISBURG, PENNSYLVANIA — This little stone building in the outskirts of the city was built in 1740, and was intended for, and was actually more than once used as, a block-house in which to take refuge in case of attack by Indians.

Ionic Capitals
HOUSE FOR ROBERT MORRIS, PHILADELPHIA, PENNSYLVANIA
G. Jardella, Sculptor

Detail of Marble Panel
HOUSE FOR ROBERT MORRIS, PHILADELPHIA, PENNSYLVANIA
G. Jardella, Sculptor

Virginia, their journeys had to be taken on horseback or in some form of vehicle. Along the traveled roads, then, that were thus created in every direction there were established after they had become stageroutes, numerous inns and taverns, many of which, being as substantially built as other buildings of the time and district, still exist, a few still serving as inns, and others converted to different uses. These inns seem generally to have been kept by English hosts, for the signboard that swung before the inn usually bore a name and painted cognizance of the same class as those that hung before many an old English inn, and we hear of "Red Lions," "White Horses," "Mariner's Compasses," "Blue Boars," "Rising Suns," and so on, in different directions. Perhaps the oldest of these inns now extant is the Jolly Post, on the Frankford Pike, built in 1680; but as the Lancaster Pike was the first turnpike road in the state, some of the many inns along its length may be older yet.

As many of these taverns are associated with historic events, and many of them, as the Paoli Inn, are extremely picturesque and interesting, a very readable monograph, illustrated with cuts of greater or less architectural value, might be founded upon them.

NEWARK, NEW JERSEY, CHURCHES

There are other parts of the Eastern seaboard than New England that can boast of graceful church spires, and in Newark, New Jersey, the spires of the Old First Presbyterian Church and Trinity Church show that the traditions of refinement and good proportion were not followed only in New England — though the designers were not over happy in uniting the wooden spires with

OAK TREE TAVERN, MONTGOMERY COUNTY, PENNSYLVANIA
Now used as a Public Hall

BLUE-BELL TAVERN, DERBY, PENNSYLVANIA

PRESBYTERIAN CHURCH—1744—NEWARK,
NEW JERSEY

TRINITY CHURCH—1805—NEWARK,
NEW JERSEY

OLD DUTCH INN, KINGSTON, NEW YORK

the stone towers. The Presbyterian Church, erected in 1774 by a society then more than one hundred years old, was much injured by fire a couple of years ago. Trinity Church, built later (1805), is interesting not only by reason of its spire, but because the designer seems not to have hesitated to use pointed and full-centered arches in the same building.

THE VANDENHEUVEL HOUSE, NEW YORK, NEW YORK

The custom of importing building materials in early days was not confined to English descendants and England. In fact, we know that Washington imported some of the materials and fittings used at Mount Vernon from the Continent, and the frequency with which the blue Dutch tile and the Dutch scenic wall paper are encountered shows that Holland was also a considerable source of supply. Perhaps, too, the use of the Flemish bond in the early brickwork may be adduced as a possible proof that not only bricks but bricklayers were of Dutch extraction. Be this as it may, there is record that when, in 1759, Cornelius Vandenheuvel, quondam Governor of Demerara, decided to build a house on the Bloomingdale Road near New York City, he imported from Holland all the material used in its construction. This house, later known as Wade's Tavern, a famous road-house in its day, still stands, though much changed outwardly, the original roof, destroyed by fire in the fifties, being replaced with a third story in wood, with a flat roof, ill according with the stone walls below.

BETHLEHEM

Although Bethlehem was founded in 1741 by Bishop Nitschmann of the Moravian Church, its name was given by Count Zinzendorf when, some years later, he visited the country to look after the well-being of the settlers whose emigration had been promoted by himself and his wife Edmuth Dorothea. The Gemeinhaus, the residence of ministers and missionaries, built in 1742, is the oldest structure in the town. It is built of logs, which since 1868 have been covered with weatherboards; but until that time the walls were protected on the outside with stucco applied over split-oak laths.

TRINITY CHURCH, NEWPORT, RHODE ISLAND

Although the spire of Trinity Church is certainly graceful, the rest of the fabric, including the tower, is so severely plain that it is doubtful whether, placed in any other town than Newport, it would ever have attracted much attention. But, thanks to its being one of the features of a fashionable summer resort, admiration for Trinity Church as a piece of architecture has become a cult, and it is probably a better-known building, architecturally speaking, than the Old South Church, Boston, itself, by and under which thousands upon thousands of unseeing eyes pass daily. Trinity was built in 1726, but by whom designed, even devoted antiquary that he was, Mr. George C. Mason, an architect of Newport, was, we believe, unable to discover. Although in 1762 the church was sawed in two and lengthened, so as to about double its original capacity, it has been carefully watched, and until the recent introduction of memorial stained-glass windows nothing had been done to impair the original effect and character of the interior finish adequately represented here.

STENTON NEAR PHILADELPHIA

It is only natural that the various patriotic orders and societies which in such numbers have sprung into being in the last decade should be mainly interested in effecting the preservation of sites and buildings that have primarily an historic significance, and a large number of the buildings that they have preserved, or

An Evening Silhouette.

· Trinity · Church · Newport · R · I ·

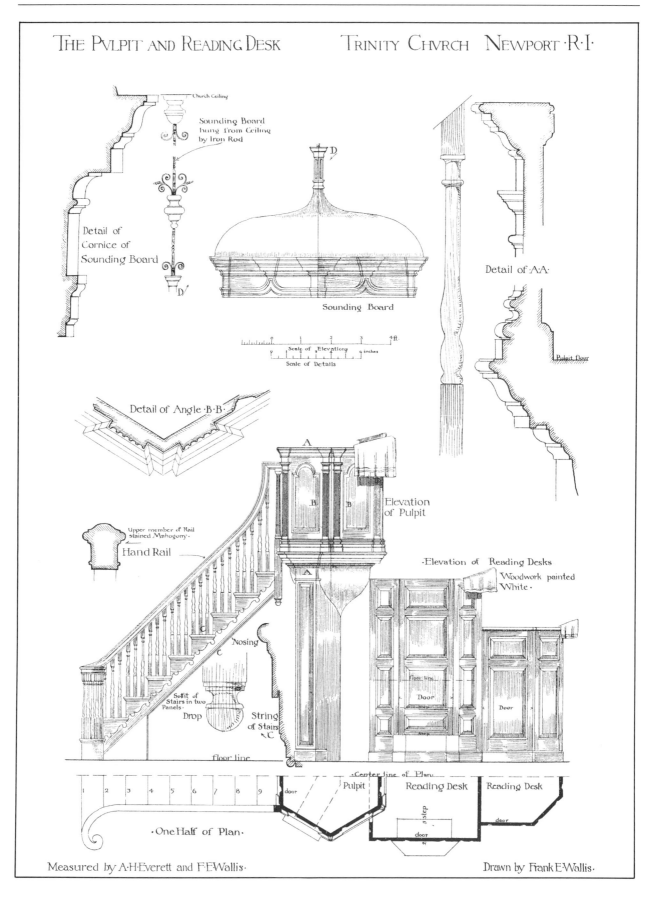

THE PVLPIT AND READING DESK   TRINITY CHVRCH NEWPORT·R·I·

Church Ceiling

Sounding Board
hung from Ceiling
by Iron Rod

Detail of
Cornice of
Sounding Board

D

D'

Sounding Board

Scale of Elevations
Scale of Details

Detail of ·A·A·

Pulpit floor

Detail of Angle ·B·B·

Upper member of Rail
stained Mahogany·

Hand Rail

Elevation
of Pulpit

·Elevation of Reading Desks·
Woodwork painted
White·

Nosing

Soffit of
Stairs in two
Panels·

Drop

String
of Stairs
·C

floor line
Door

Door

floor line

Center line of Plan·

One Half of Plan·

door

Pulpit

Reading Desk

Reading Desk

door

Measured by A·H·Everett and F·E·Wallis·   Drawn by Frank E·Wallis·

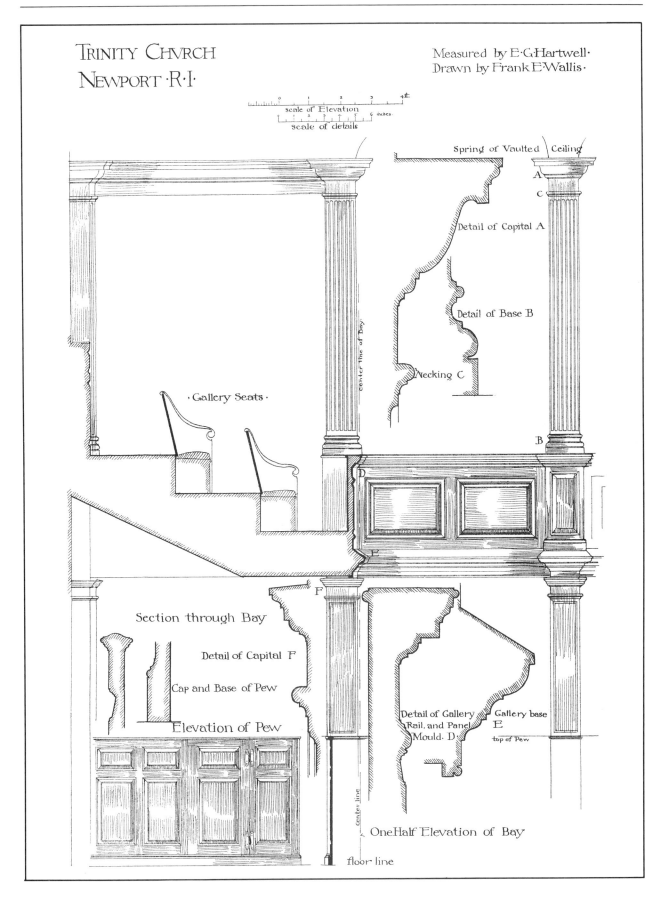

TRINITY CHVRCH
NEWPORT · R · I ·

Measured by E·G·Hartwell·
Drawn by Frank E·Wallis·

scale of Elevation
scale of details

Spring of Vaulted Ceiling

A
C

Detail of Capital A

Detail of Base B

Necking C

· Gallery Seats ·

center line of Bay

B

D

E

F

Section through Bay

Detail of Capital F

Cap and Base of Pew

Elevation of Pew

Detail of Gallery
Rail, and Panel
Mould. D

Gallery base
E
top of Pew

center line

One Half Elevation of Bay

floor line

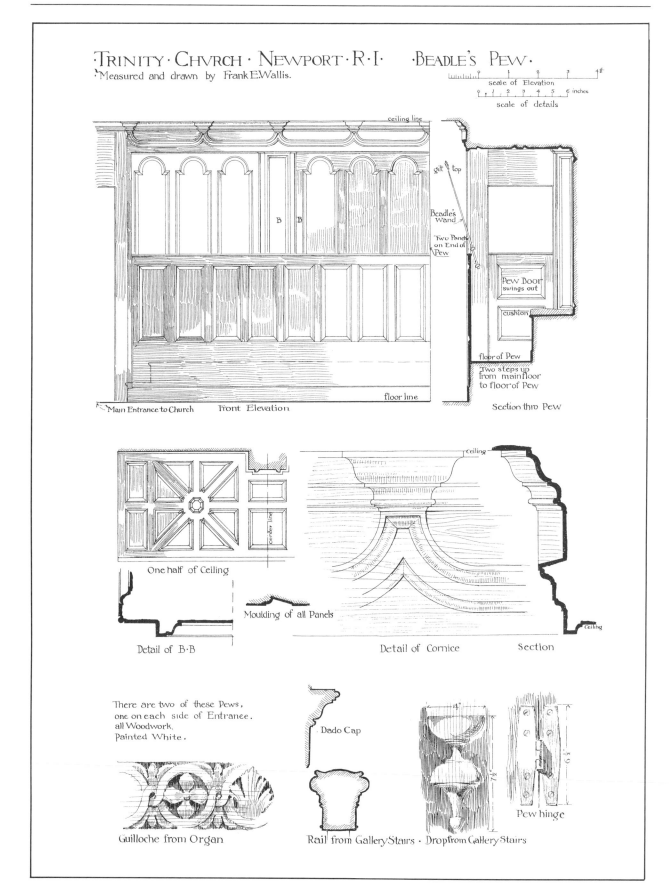

·TRINITY·CHVRCH·NEWPORT·R·I·   ·BEADLE'S PEW·
·Measured and drawn by Frank E.Wallis.

scale of Elevation
scale of details

ceiling line

B B

gilt top

Beadle's Wand

Two Panels on End of Pew

Pew Door swings out

cushion

floor of Pew

Two steps up from main floor to floor of Pew

floor line.

Main Entrance to Church   Front Elevation

Section thro Pew

One half of Ceiling

ceiling

center line

Moulding of all Panels

Detail of B·B

Detail of Cornice   Section

There are two of these Pews,
one on each side of Entrance.
all Woodwork,
Painted White.

Dado Cap

Guilloche from Organ

Rail from Gallery Stairs · Drop from Gallery Stairs

Pew hinge

STENTON — 1728 — NEAR PHILADELPHIA,
PENNSYLVANIA

Home of James Logan

by a tablet have indicated the original site thereof, have absolutely no architectural value. To offset these now and then one is preserved which should have had the fostering care of someone, and the fortuitous happening that a building of architectural worth owes its preservation to the accidents of history rather than to its deserts as the outcome of artistic effort makes us none the less grateful to those who have accomplished it, no matter whether respect for history, pride of family or love of art were the motive.

The Society of Colonial Dames of Pennsylvania, which furnishes the illustrations on page 00, a year or two ago secured the right to restore and preserve Stenton, the house built in 1728 by James Logan, first secretary to William Penn and later Secretary of the Province, President of the Council, Acting Governor of the Province and Chief Justice of the Supreme Court of Pennsylvania for many years.

Its right to preservation as the scene of many an historic incident is as little to be questioned as that of its value as a signpost on our road of architectural progress.

Detail of Entrance
STENTON — 1728 — NEAR PHILADELPHIA,
PENNSYLVANIA

House built by John Bartram (the botanist) at Gray's Bay. Phila.

Built 1730.

Sketches for July 19   Frank C. Hays

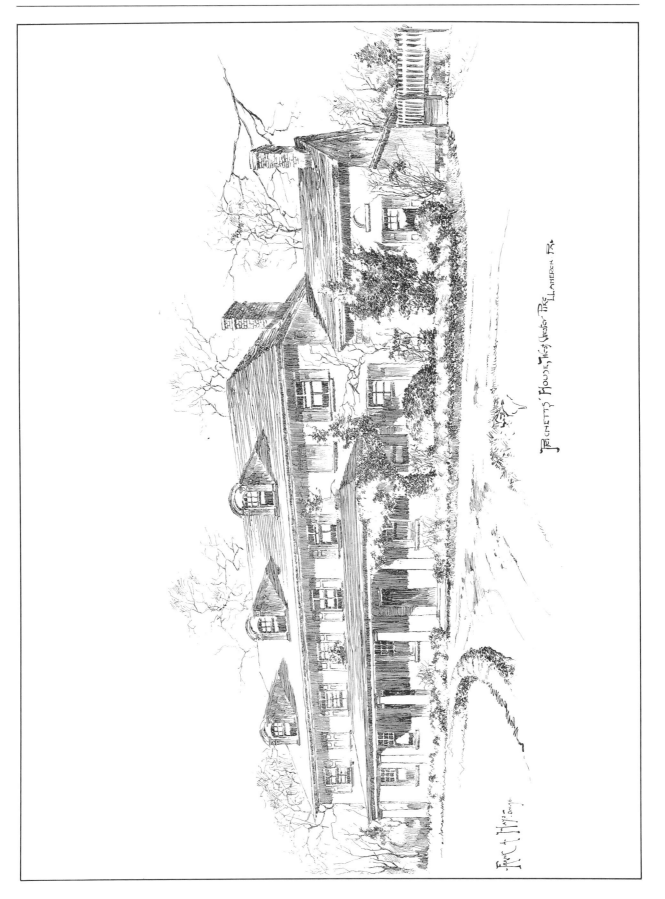

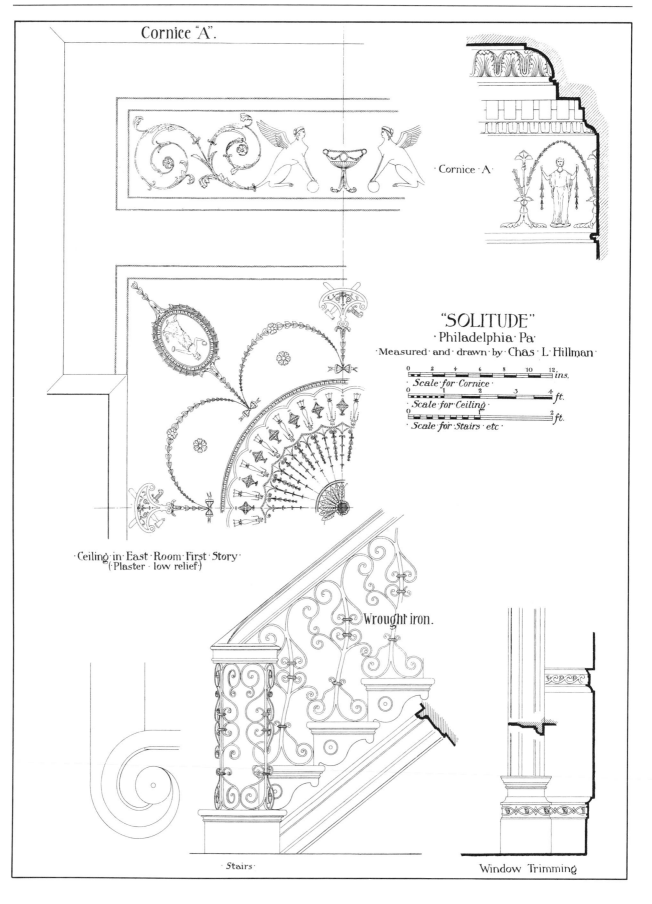

Cornice "A".

·Cornice·A·

"SOLITUDE"
·Philadelphia·Pa·
·Measured·and·drawn·by·Chas·L·Hillman·

· Scale·for·Cornice ·
· Scale·for·Ceiling ·
· Scale·for·Stairs·etc ·

·Ceiling·in·East·Room·First·Story·
(·Plaster·low·relief·)

Wrought iron.

·Stairs·

Window Trimming

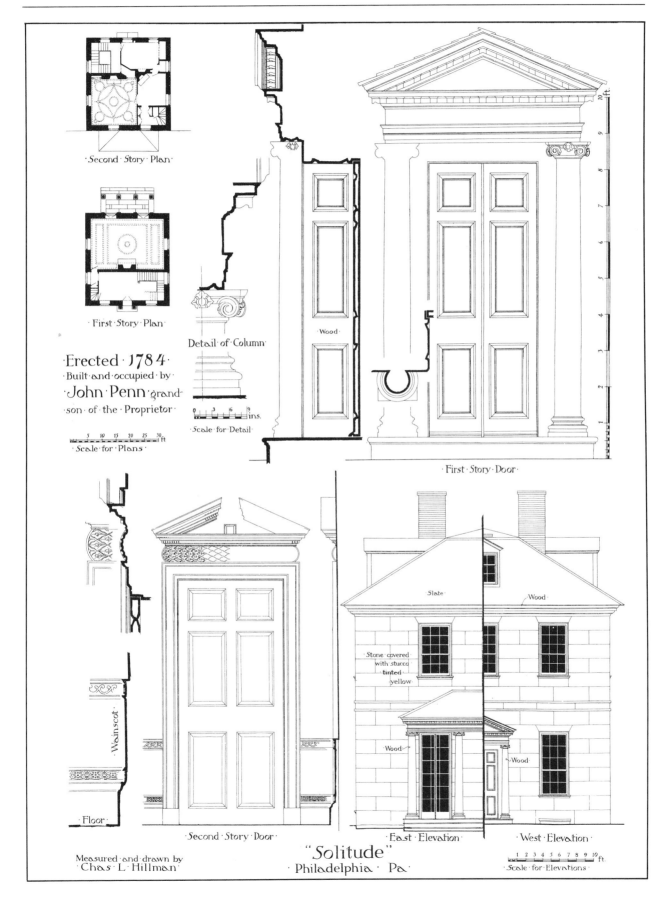

·Second·Story·Plan·

·First·Story·Plan·

Erected·1784·
·Built·and·occupied·by·
·John·Penn·grand-
·son·of·the·Proprietor·

5 10 15 20 25 30 ft
·Scale·for·Plans·

Detail·of·Column·

0 3 6 9 ins.
·Scale·for·Detail·

Wood

·First·Story·Door·

Wainscot

Floor

·Second·Story·Door·

Slate

Wood

Stone·covered
with·stucco
tinted
yellow

Wood

Wood

·East·Elevation·

·West·Elevation·

Measured·and·drawn·by
·Chas·L·Hillman·

"Solitude"
·Philadelphia·Pa·

1 2 3 4 5 6 7 8 9 10 ft
·Scale·for·Elevations·

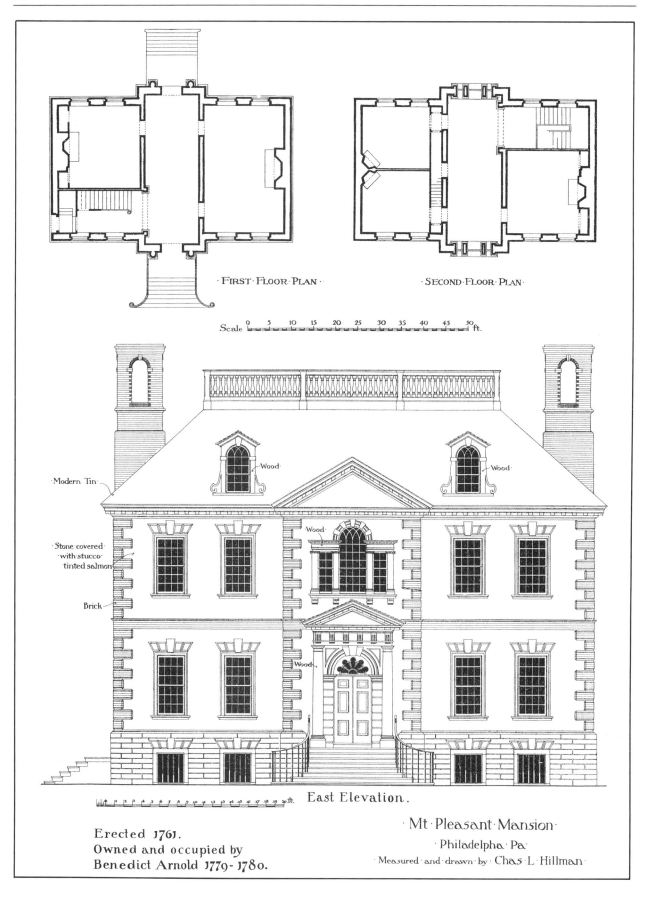

·FIRST·FLOOR·PLAN·   ·SECOND·FLOOR·PLAN·

Scale 0 5 10 15 20 25 30 35 40 45 50 ft.

·Modern Tin·

·Stone·covered·
·with·stucco·
·tinted·salmon·

·Brick·

·Wood·   ·Wood·

·Wood·

·Wood·

East Elevation.

Erected 1761.
Owned and occupied by
Benedict Arnold 1779-1780.

·Mt·Pleasant·Mansion·
·Philadelpha·Pa·
·Measured·and·drawn·by·Chas·L·Hillman·

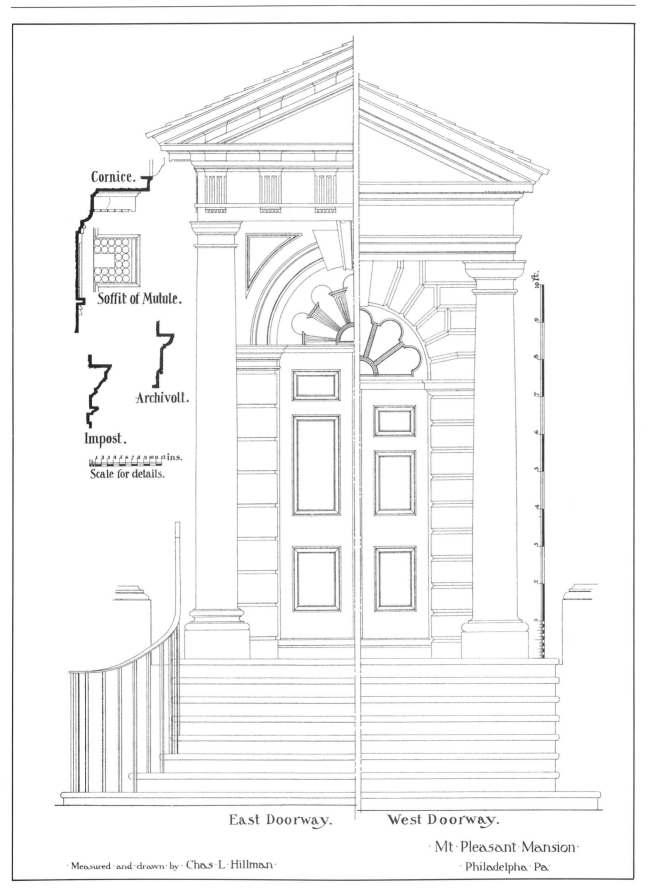

Cornice.

Soffit of Mutule.

Archivolt.

Impost.

Scale for details.

East Doorway. · · West Doorway.

· Mt · Pleasant · Mansion ·

· Philadelpha · Pa ·

· Measured · and · drawn · by · Chas · L · Hillman ·

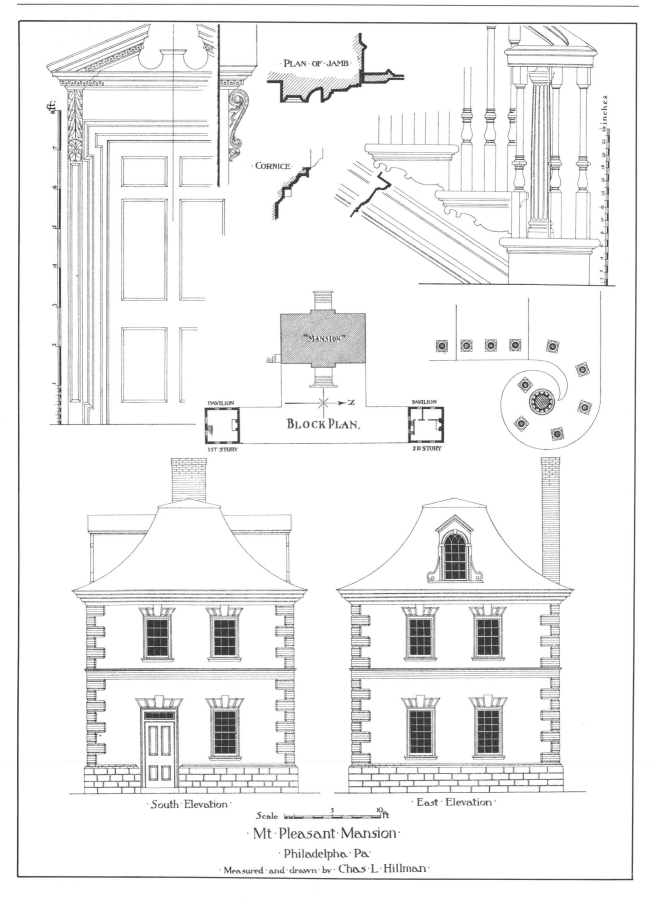

PLAN·OF·JAMB

·CORNICE·

8 ft.

24 inches

"MANSION"

PAVILION

BLOCK PLAN.

PAVILION

1ST STORY

2D STORY

·South·Elevation·

·East·Elevation·

Scale   5   10 ft

·Mt·Pleasant·Mansion·

·Philadelpha·Pa·

·Measured·and·drawn·by·Chas·L·Hillman·

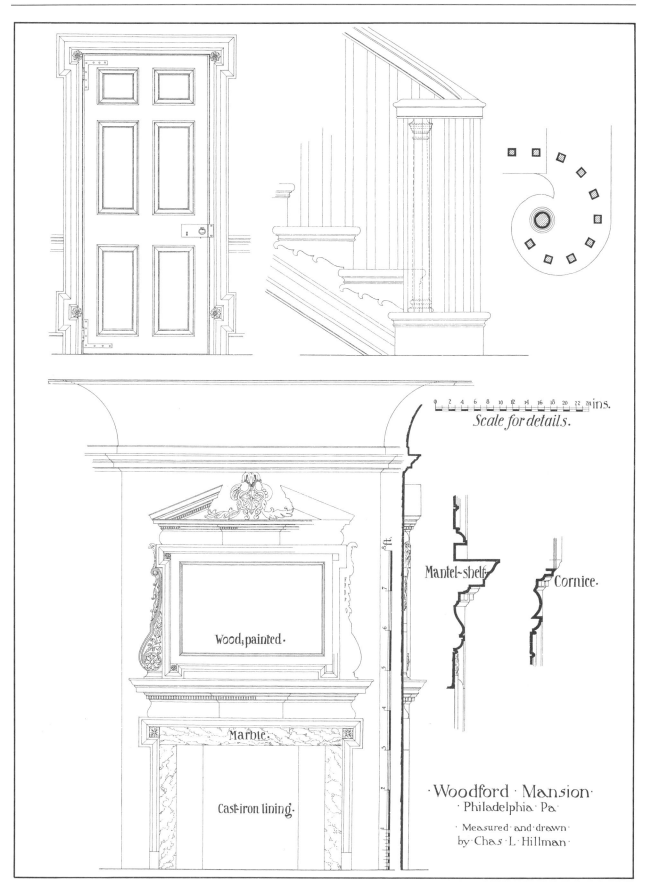

Scale for details.

Mantel~shelf.

Cornice.

Wood, painted.

Marble.

Cast-iron lining.

·Woodford · Mansion·
· Philadelphia · Pa·

· Measured · and · drawn ·
by · Chas · L · Hillman

ARNOLD'S MANSION
FAIRMOUNT PARK PHILADA

Frank A Hays June 93

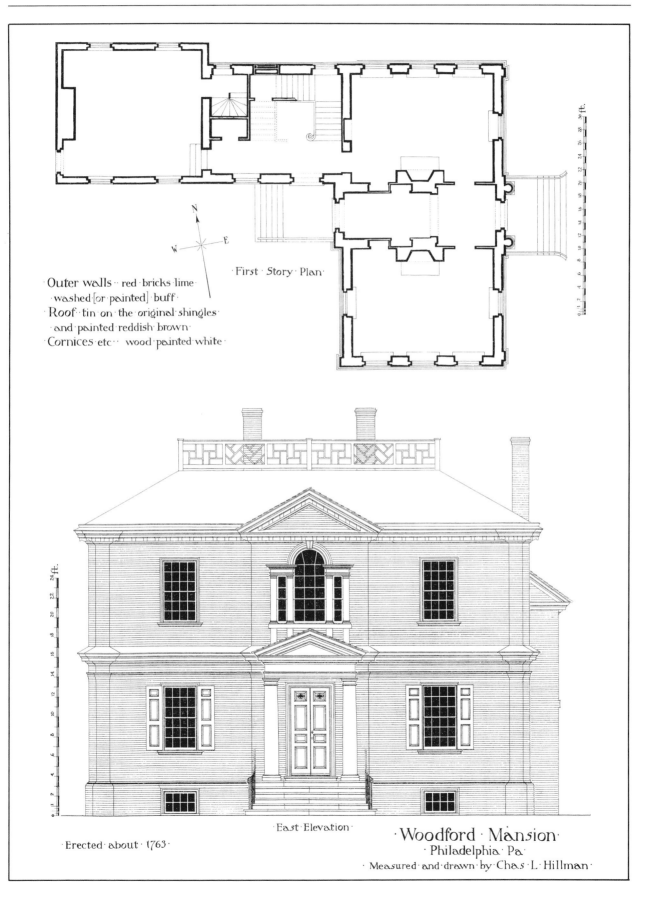

First · Story · Plan ·

·Outer walls ·· red ·bricks ·lime·
·washed [or painted] ·buff·
·Roof· tin· on· the· original· shingles·
·and· painted· reddish· brown·
·Cornices· etc·· wood ·painted ·white·

· East ·Elevation·

· Erected· about· 1763 ·

·Woodford · Mansion·
·Philadelphia· Pa·
· Measured· and· drawn· by· Chas · L· Hillman·

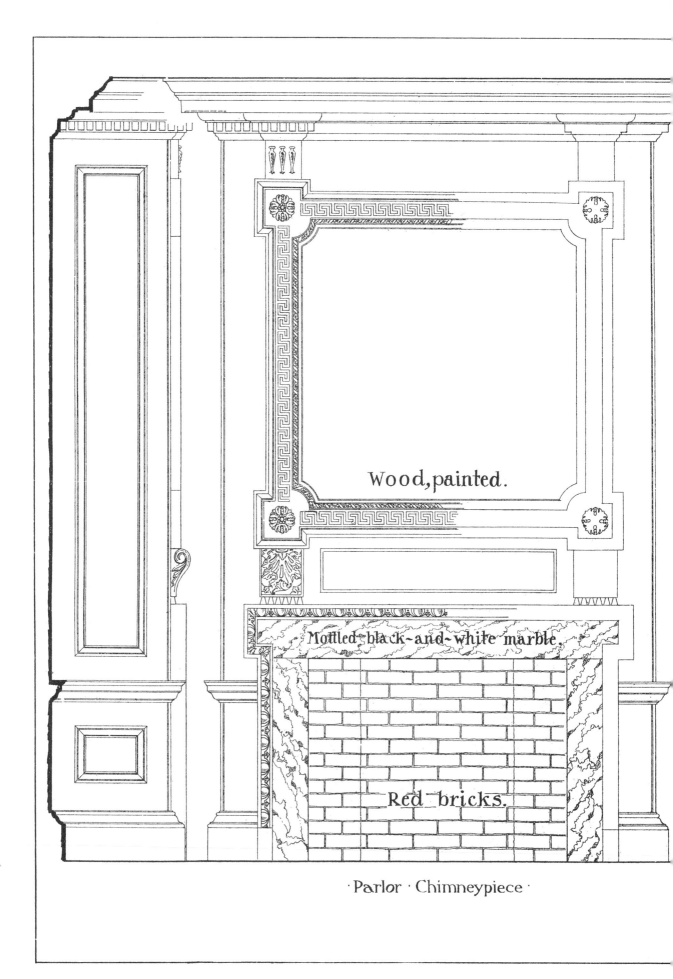

Wood, painted.

Mottled black-and-white marble.

Red bricks.

· Parlor · Chimneypiece ·

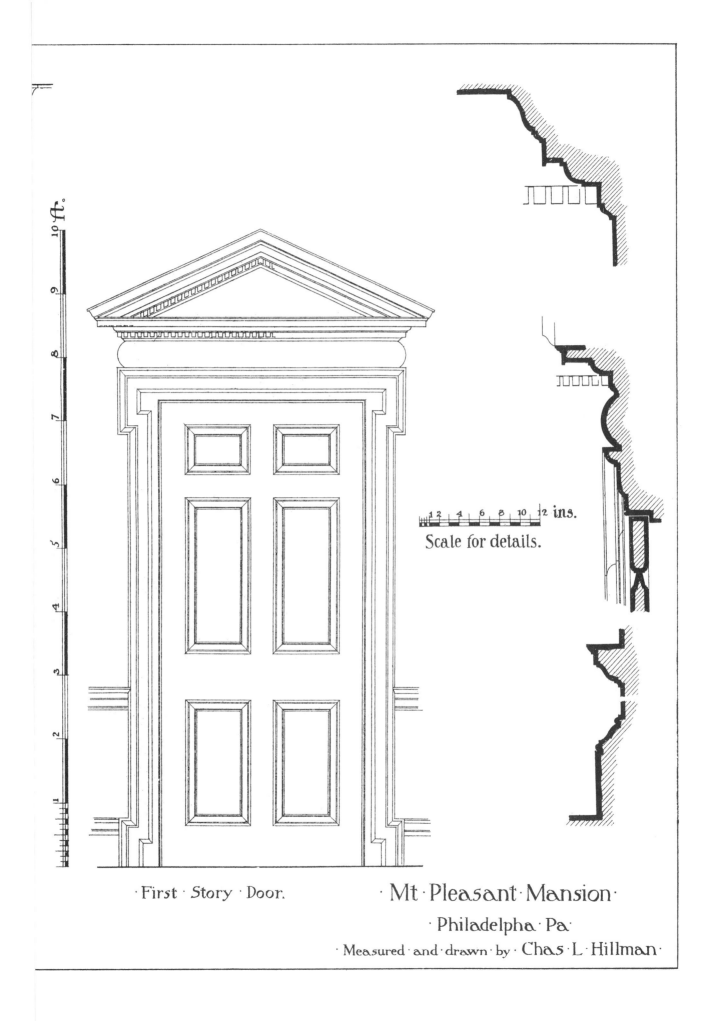

·First·Story·Door.

10 Ft.

Scale for details.

Mt·Pleasant·Mansion·

·Philadelpha·Pa·

·Measured·and·drawn·by·Chas·L·Hillman·

TWO OLD PHILADELPHIA CHURCHES

ST. PETER'S P. E. CHURCH

IT is a real disappointment to find that the feature which makes St. Peter's P. E. Church, on the corner of Third and Pine streets, Philadelphia, so unusually picturesque is not coeval with the original church, or chapel, structure. The upper part of the square tower, with its slender octagonal spire telescoping behind the battlemented roof, was added to the original chapel, in 1842, by the well-known architect William Strickland, in order to receive a chime of bells presented about that time by some friend of the parish.

In 1758, the vestry of Christ Church, finding the structure that had been begun only thirty years before already too small to accommodate the increasing number of those who would worship there, record that "it is unanimously agreed that another church is much wanted; and it is proposed that the taking and collecting the subscriptions and conducting the affairs relating to the building, and furnishing the said intended church, shall be under the management of the minister, church wardens and vestry of Christ Church."

As a chapel, then, of Christ Church, St. Peter's was built, between 1758–1761, and maintained until 1832, when a separation from the parent body was effected.

The site was granted by the "honorable proprietaries," and on it was built of brick a structure 60' x 90' and crowned at one end by a small cupola in which hung two small bells. From the differences between the color and character of the brickwork of the upper and lower portions of the tower, it appears likely that the lower part of the tower is part of the original structure and that Strickland added to it the upper part and the spire.

GLORIA DEI, OR OLD SWEDES CHURCH

"Thus, through God's blessing, we have completed the great work and have built a church superior to any in this country, so that the English themselves, who now govern this Province, and are beyond measure richer than we are, wonder at what we have done."

In the above words Pastor Bjork wrote home to Sweden in 1700, so that his superiors in the Swedish National Church might know what had been accomplished and the successors of Gustave Adolphus might know how the Swedish colonists, who emigrated to the country in conformity with a plan conceived by that king, were prospering. Probably many who regard with amiable approbation the important place held by Scandinavians in the tabulations of the annual influx of immigrants of late years do not know that the Swedes are really amongst our oldest settlers. Their settlement at Wecacoe — now Philadelphia — antedates the arrival of William Penn (the Tinicum Church, the predecessor of the present structure, being built in 1642), and Penn is said to have merely adopted in his dealings with the Indians the methods already practiced by the Swedes.

Although there are older church societies in the country and some of these have been able to celebrate their two hundred-and-fiftieth anniversary, the original structures in which their worship began have long since vanished and there are not many church fabrics in the country, not even the Spanish mission chapels in Texas, that can boast longer life than Gloria Dei, more familiarly known as the Old Swedes Church on Swanson Street, Philadelphia. Further than this, there is probably no parish that has worshipped uninterruptedly in the same building for so many years. Gloria Dei has never closed its doors, and in this it outranks the slightly older Swedish church that was built at Christina — now Wilmington, Delaware.

In 1900 Gloria Dei will celebrate the two hundredth anniversary of the completion of the church building and the two hundred and twenty-third anniversary of the formation of the Society. During the first hundred years of its existence the rites of the Swedish National Church were practiced, but by the end of that time the Swedes had become thorough Americans, spoke English and no longer felt the closeness of the tie that connected them with their mother country, and so declined longer to receive the native Swedish pastors sent over from time to time. During the last hundred years the parish has been affiliated with the Protestant Episcopal Church.

The baptismal font is said to have been brought from Sweden by the early colonists, who used it in their service in the original church structure — the converted block-house that then stood where the church now stands. The bell, too, is recast from the old bell used in 1643, and bears the couplet: —

"I to the church the living call,
And to the grave do summon all."

"OLD SWEDES' CHURCH."
Philadelphia, Pa.

Jamb.

Cornice.

SOUTH DOOR.

Scale for details.

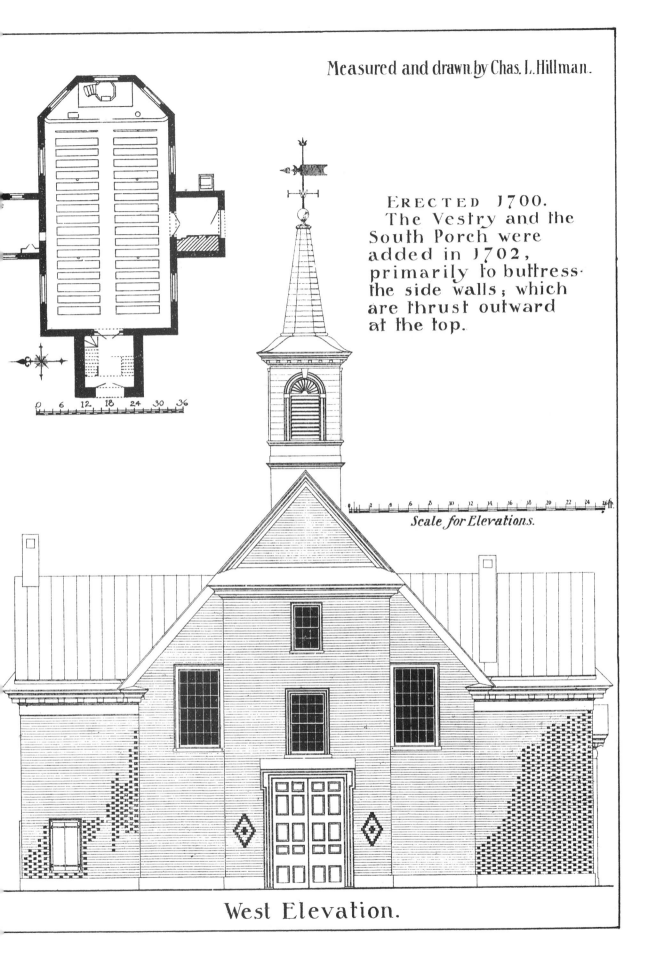

Measured and drawn by Chas. L. Hillman.

ERECTED 1700.
The Vestry and the
South Porch were
added in 1702,
primarily to buttress·
the side walls; which
are thrust outward
at the top.

0 6 12 18 24 30 36

Scale for Elevations.

West Elevation.

GLORIA DEI (OLD SWEDES CHURCH)—1700—
SWANSON STREET, PHILADELPHIA,
PENNSYLVANIA

ST. PETER'S P. E. CHURCH—1758–1761—THIRD AND
PINE STREETS, PHILADELPHIA, PENNSYLVANIA

Interior
ST. PETER'S P. E. CHURCH — 1758–1761 — THIRD AND
PINE STREETS, PHILADELPHIA, PENNSYLVANIA

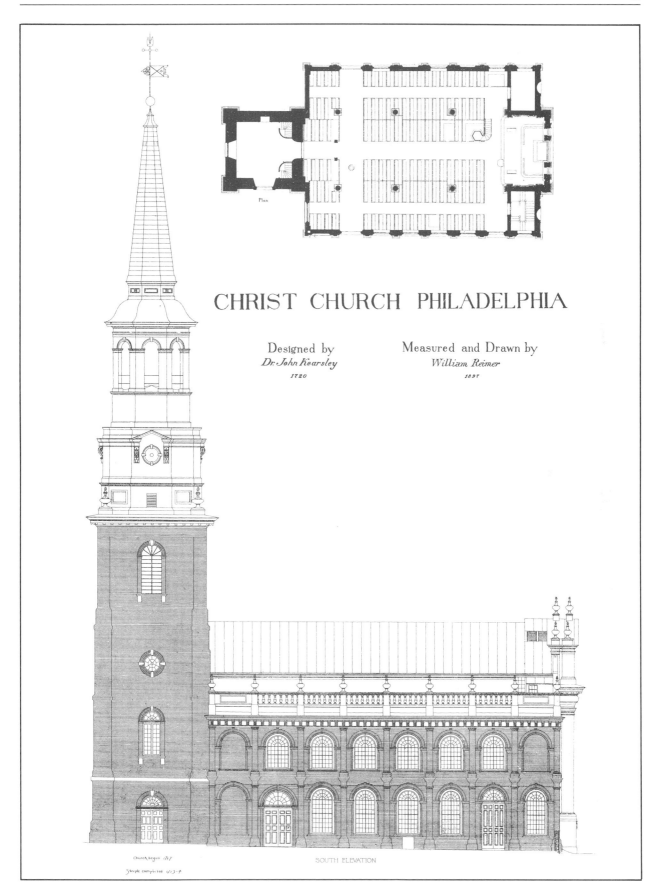

CHRIST CHURCH PHILADELPHIA

Designed by
Dr. John Kearsley
1720

Measured and Drawn by
William Reimer
1897

SOUTH ELEVATION

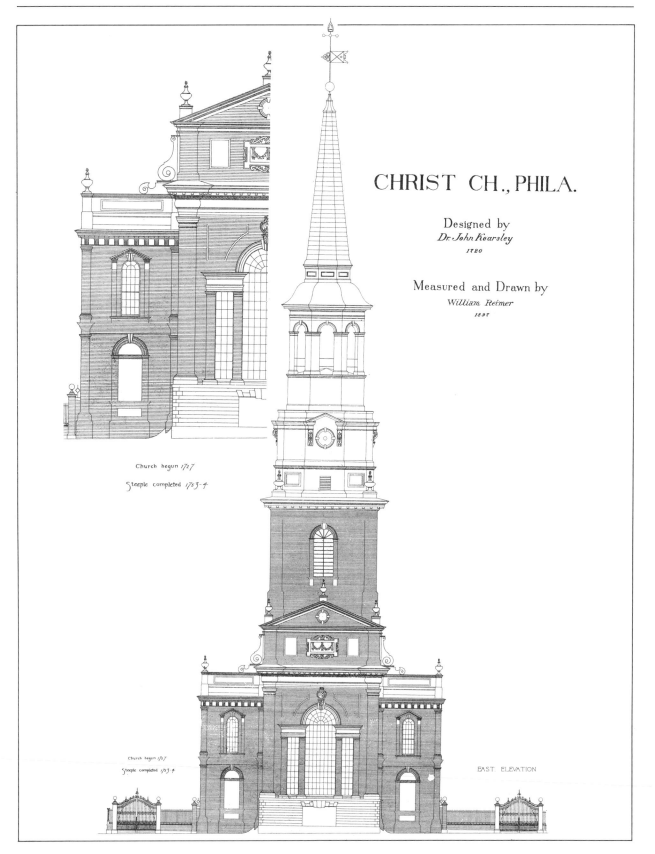

CHRIST CH., PHILA.

Designed by
Dr. John Kearsley
1720

Measured and Drawn by
William Reimer
1897

Church begun 1727

Steeple completed 1753-4

Church begun 1727

Steeple completed 1753-4

EAST ELEVATION

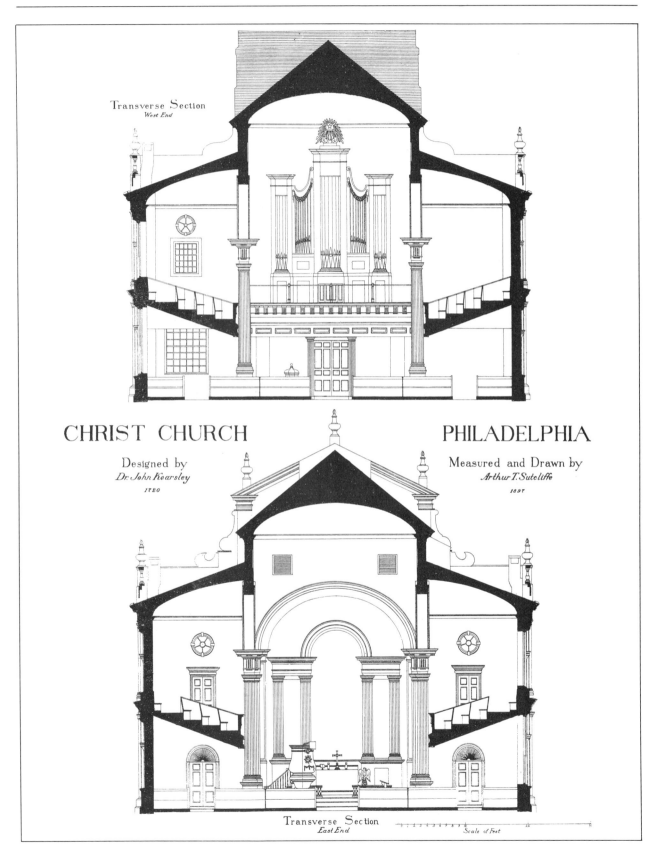

Transverse Section
West End

CHRIST CHURCH   PHILADELPHIA

Designed by   Measured and Drawn by
Dr. John Kearsley   Arthur T. Sutcliffe
1720   1897

Transverse Section
East End

Scale of Feet

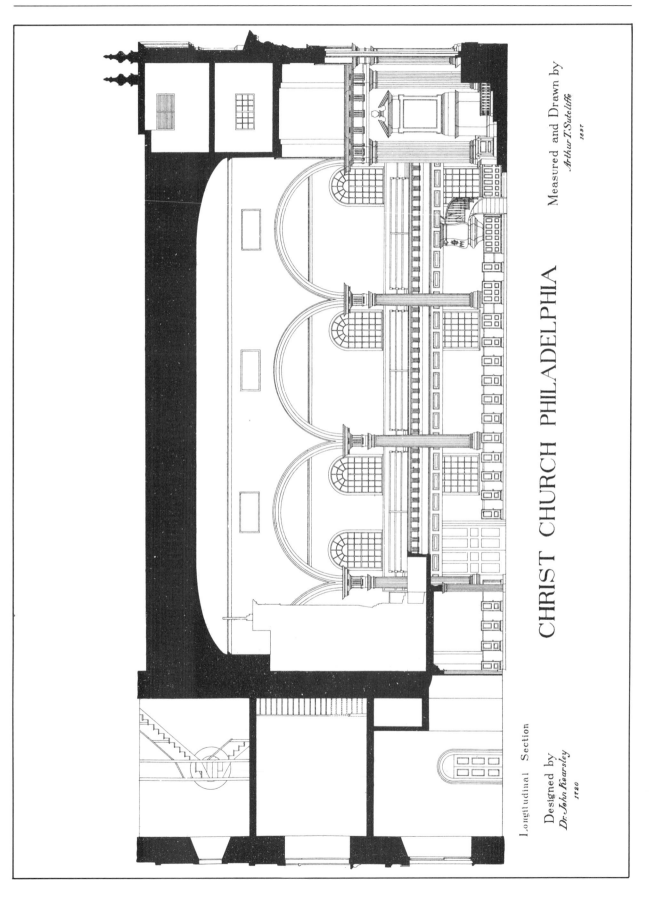

CHRIST CHURCH PHILADELPHIA

Measured and Drawn by
Arthur T. Sutcliffe
1897

Longitudinal Section

Designed by
Dr. John Kearsley
1720

Verplanck Homestead,
Fishkill, New York

Text by
A. J. Bloor
Originally published in 1898 as
Volume I of The Georgian Period

VERPLANCK HOMESTEAD AT FISHKILL,
HUDSON RIVER, NEW YORK

THE VERPLANCK HOMESTEAD, FISHKILL, NEW YORK

THE Verplanck homestead stands on the lands granted by the Wappinger Indians, in 1683, to Gulian Verplanck and Francis Rombout, under a license given by Governor Thomas Dongan, Commander-in-Chief of the province of New York, and confirmed, in 1685, by letters-patent from the King, James II. The purchase included "all that Tract or Parcell of land Scituate on the East side of Hudson's river, beginning from the South side of a Creek called the fresh Kill and by the Indians Mattewan, and from thence Northward along said Hudson's river five hundred Rodd beyond the Great Wappin's Kill, and from thence into the woods fouer Houres goeing"; or, in our speech, easterly sixteen English miles. There were eighty-five thousand acres in this grant, and the "Schedull or Perticuler" of money and goods given to the natives, in exchange, by Francis Rumbout and Gulyne Ver Planke sounds oddly today:

One hundred Royalls,
One hundred Pound Powder,
Two hundred fathom of white Wampum,
One hundred Barrs of lead,
One hundred fathom of black Wampum,
Thirty tobacco boxes, ten holl adzes,
Thirty Gunns, twenty Blankets,
Forty fathom of Duffils,
Twenty fathom of stroudwater Cloth,
Thirty Kittles, forty Hatchets,
Forty Hornes, forty Shirts,
Forty pair stockins,
Twelve coates of B. C.,
Ten drawing Knives,
Forty earthen Juggs,
Forty Bottles, Fouer ankers Rum,
Forty Knives, ten halfe Vatts Beere,
Two hundred tobacco pipes,
Eighty pound tobacco

The purchasers were also to pay Governor Dongan six bushels of good and merchantable winter wheat every year. The deed is recorded at Albany in Volume 5 of the Book of Patents.

Before 1685 Gulian Verplanck died, leaving minor children, and settlements on his portion of the land were thus postponed. Divisions of the estate were made in 1708, in 1722, and again in 1740. It is not accurately known when the homestead, the present low Dutch farmhouse was built, but we know that it stood where it now stands, before the Revolutionary War, and the date commonly assigned to the building is a little before 1740.

The house stands on a bluff overlooking the Hudson, about a mile and one-half north of Fishkill Landing. It is one-story and one-half high, of stone, plastered. The gambrel roof is shingled, descends low and has dormer windows. The house has always been occupied and is in excellent preservation. Baron Steuben chose it for his headquarters, no doubt for its nearness to Washington's headquarters across the river, and for the beauty and charm of the situation. It is made still further famous by the fact that under its roof was organized, in 1783, the Society of the Cincinnati. The room then used is on the right of the hall, and is carefully preserved. In fancy we can picture the assembly of officers grouped about Washington, in that west room overlooking the river, pledging themselves to preserve the memories of the years during which they had struggled for their country's being.

On May 20, 1899, there was unveiled with appropriate ceremonies a tablet placed on this house by the Colonial Dames of the State of New York. The inscription on this tablet reads:—

MOUNT GULIAN
Built about 1740 by
GULIAN VER PLANCK
GRANDSON OF GULIAN VER PLANCK
WHO PURCHASED THE ADJACENT LAND

FROM THE WAPPINGER INDIANS IN 1683.

HEADQUARTERS OF BARON VON STEUBEN
THE SOCIETY OF THE CINCINNATI WAS
Instituted here May, 1783.

PLACED BY THE COLONIAL DAMES
OF THE STATE OF NEW YORK
MDCCCXCIX

VIRTUTE MAJORUM FILLAE CONSERVANT.

The whole neighborhood, especially the village of Fishkill, which was the principal settlement in the county at that date, has many Revolutionary associations. The interior army route to Boston passed through the village; this was a depot of army stores, and workshops and hospitals were established. Here was forged the sword of Washington, now in the keeping of the United States Government, and exhibited in the late Centennial collection. It is marked with the maker's name, J. Bailey, Fishkill.

The New York Legislature, retiring before the approach of the British, after the evacuation of the city, came at last to Fishkill, and here the constitution of the state was printed, in 1777, on the press of Samuel Loundon, the first book, Lossing says, ever printed in the state.

Some years after peace was restored, the Verplanck family appear to have occupied the homestead from time to time. Philip Verplanck, a grandson of Gulian, the original grantee, was a native of the Patent, but his public life was spent elsewhere. He was an engineer and surveyor, and an able man. Verplanck's Point in Westchester County, where Fort Lafayette stood during the Revolution, was named for him, and he represented that Manor in the Colonial Assembly from 1734 to 1768. Finally, Daniel Crommelin Verplanck with his large family—one of his sons being the well-known Gulian C. Verplanck, born here in 1786—came to live in the old home permanently. He had led an active life in New York, served in Congress and on the bench, and now retired to the quiet of the country. It was he who planted the fine old trees which now shade the lawn; among them the coffee tree so much admired. About 1810 the north end, built of wood, was added to the old house. Architects were not numerous, apparently, in those days, so the Dutch type was lost in making this large addition, though the interior is quaint, dignified and interesting. It was from under its roof that Daniel C. Verplanck was carried to his last restingplace as his father before him, and generations after him lived and still live in the old homestead.

For the above descriptions prepared with no little painstaking, of an interesting house and demesne, as well as for the loan of the photograph from which I made my pen-and-ink sketch of it, I am wholly indebted to a member of the Verplanck family and a mutual friend.

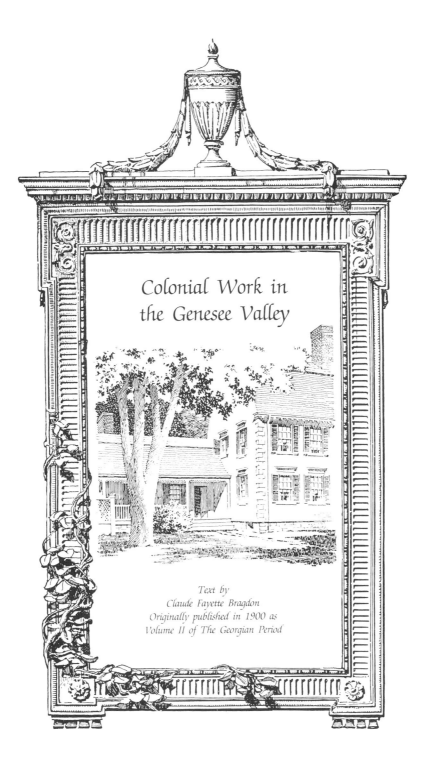

Colonial Work in
the Genesee Valley

Text by
Claude Fayette Bragdon
Originally published in 1900 as
Volume II of The Georgian Period

Front Porch
CULVER HOMESTEAD, BRIGHTON, MONROE
COUNTY, NEW YORK

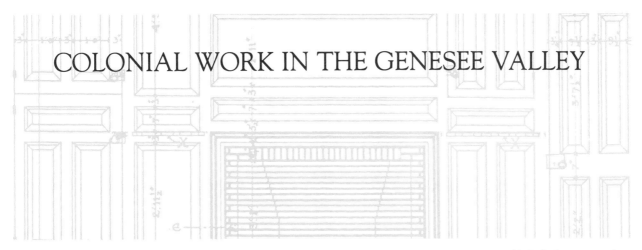

COLONIAL WORK IN THE GENESEE VALLEY

IN all America there is hardly to be found a fairer or more fertile region than that part of New York State embraced in what is known as the Phelps and Gorham purchase—the "park-like Genesee Country," as Mrs. Van Rensselaer has most felicitously called it. The Senecas, whose villages and yellow cornfields once lay thick on either side of the broad, fordable river, gave it the name of the Beautiful Valley, and surely none could be more fitting.

Rising in the precipitous region south of Portage, the Genesee, in its first miles, pursues a tortuous course between narrow banks, until, in the vicinity of Mount Morris (whose Indian name meant "where the river forsakes the hills"), it enters a broad, undulating country, part clear, part wooded, and gemmed by many crystal lakes. At Rochester it attains the level of Ontario by means of two high cataracts, and for the remaining few miles of its course flows slowly and soberly between the confining walls of the famous gorge of the Genesee.

The beautiful country drained by this noble river has been, from the earliest times, a favorite dwelling place of man. Far in the past, it was the center and stronghold of the Iroquois nation—those Romans of the ancient American world. The first white faces that appeared to them there came probably from France— devoted Jesuit missionaries and adventurous *coureurs du bois*, to whom the region of the Great Lakes, even beyond the Mississippi, was already familiar ground when, by the Dutch and English on the coast, all west of Albany was still referred to as the "great unknown country." The French, however, never made secure their foothold on these shores, and it was, after all, the English who, by purchase and treaty, supplemented by a liberal and judicious use of firewater, dispossessed the aborigines and, in the slow course of time, evolved the average American of today.

The Falls of the Genesee, situated as they are between the Hudson River and the great cataract of

Niagara (to which they are a hardly inferior spectacle), have in the past attracted many illustrious visitors. Louis Philippe with some members of his court followed the Indian trail from Canandaigua to the falls; Aaron Burr stopped there on one of his western journeys, and in later times came Webster, and Lafayette, and a host of others, drawn not now by the falls themselves, but by the city that had grown upon its brink. So singular is the law which governs posthumous greatness, the only two individuals connected with the locality whose names shine with sufficient luster to pierce the darkness of obscuring years are Mary Jemison, "the white woman of the Genesee," who, by remaining true to her race and loyal to her adopters, rendered inestimable service to the cause of civilization; and a gin-drinking mountebank, Sam Patch, who in his last utterance enriched the language with a new catch phrase, "Some things can be done as well as others," and jumped to his death from the upper falls, in the presence of a crowd of horror-stricken spectators.

Of the present condition and aspect of the Genesee country it is almost superfluous to speak. Rochester, though not the oldest, is the largest city, the center of what is said to be the richest agricultural district in the world. At the Western New York State Fair, held there annually, the impossible pictures of fruit and stock and poultry, made familiar through the columns of the *Homestead* and *Henhouse* and similar publica-

OLD ROCHESTER MARKET, ROCHESTER,
NEW YORK
Now destroyed

Front Porch
SMITH HOUSE, BRIGHTON, NEW YORK

tions come near to being realized — dogs with blood in their eye, chickens with whiskers on their legs and pigs so fat their feet have become mere rudimentary appendages, far up their sides. Rochester is also noted for its nurseries and fine collections of orchids, chrysanthemums and other flowers; and the many famous stables and kennels in the city and up the valley annually send representatives to metropolitan horse and bench shows.

At Genesee, Mount Morris and vicinity, there exists a condition of things common enough abroad, but rarely found in America, a sort of enlightened feudal system, the land being almost exclusively owned by a few individuals, hereditary holders, who, instead of leaving its management in the hands of unscrupulous agents and living elsewhere on the desired revenue, plant themselves squarely in the center of their own acres and identify their interests with those of their tenants. The life of the people of this class is not unlike that of the English country gentleman; their work consists in the management and improvement of their land, the bettering of the condition of the farming population and the breeding and maintaining of thoroughbred animals, preëminently the horse. Their relaxation is found in the entertainment of guests, the exchange of visits and, more than all else, fox-hunting in its season. Once every year, lured by the Genesee Valley Hunt, one of the most famous in the country, "Society" comes farther westward than is its wont, and finds in the autumnal splendors of the valley a rival to its own Berkshire Hills. Mention must be made, also, of another class whose presence colors — or discolors — the social life of several of the villages — invalids, who, seeking to renew their health from springs famous

since Indian times for their medicinal properties, are rested and often restored by a residence in so fine a climate, amid such beautiful surroundings. The mingling of these various elements renders the summer life of the valley quite distinctive, so that the curious stranger, looking from the car window, expecting to see only representatives of the rural population waiting for the incoming train, is quite as likely to be greeted by the sight of smart traps and liveried servants and well-groomed men and women, surrounded by all that they can muster of the pomp and circumstance of wealth.

I have delayed thus long in coming to the subject of the Colonial architecture of this region, because there is so little to be said, and because drawings say that little so much more completely than words. So far as I have been able to gather, from research and observation, what Colonial work the valley contains derives more from the South than from New England, which is accounted for by the fact that the first settlers came from Maryland. Many of the very oldest houses exhibit a central mass flanked by two low wings, and often a pillared portico in front (not to be confused with the Greek temple type of a later day), two features common in Southern Colonial work, but rare in Eastern. The details, too, incline to heaviness rather than to that extreme delicacy one sees in Salem and Ports-

Front Entrance
GRIFFITH HOUSE, ROCHESTER, NEW YORK
Now destroyed

LEADED GLASS FORMS,
ROCHESTER, NEW YORK

hered to, and this ended in the unrelieved hopelessness of "carpenters' Classic."

Of Colonial architecture, properly so-called, Rochester affords few examples, such as may once have existed, nearly all having been demolished to give place to new work. There remain, however, scattered throughout the city many beautiful doorways, cornices and other bits of detail, and leaded glasswork of fine design in variety and profusion. In the older residence section there are some good houses dating from that period when the Greek influence was beginning to supplant the Palladian, and of these I may mention a doorway of the Nehemiah Osborne House (now owned and occupied by the Security Trust Company), which, though not strictly Colonial, is yet a most original and beautiful application of Greek ornament to American conditions.

In Canandaigua there exist conditions more favorable to the preservation of its past architecture and it is accordingly rich in good material left by the ebbing tide of prosperity. The village, situated on the shore of the lake of the same name, is one of the oldest in the state and was long regarded as the farthest outpost of civilization. On the consummation of the Phelps and Gorham purchase in the summer of 1788, a land office, the first in America, was opened there by Mr. Phelps,

LIVINGSTON PARK SEMINARY,
ROCHESTER, NEW YORK

mouth houses. A Dutch influence, derived from Albany and New York, the then nearest large cities, may be seen in many of the old doorways and in "spindley" mantels with fan-shaped ornaments. The architecture here passed through the same phases as elsewhere throughout the country; an increasing heaviness and coarseness led at last to the adoption of Greek ornament and proportioning, more and more slavishly ad-

BLOCK OF HOUSES, GENEVA, NEW YORK

for the sale of the land to settlers, who shortly came swarming from the east to buy and occupy it. Early in the town's history, Louis Philippe, escaping from the storm which rocked the thrones of Europe, settled in Canandaigua with a few followers, and, in the heart of a virgin wilderness, inhabited by fierce, and sometimes hostile, savages, established a toy court over which he ruled, a make-believe monarch.

The village consists mainly of one street, but that is a magnificent one, lined and intersected by long rows of large trees. The houses, old and stately, set far back and far apart, each in the center of well-kept grounds. The tone of the place is eminently aristocratic and this is enhanced by the existence of two large private schools, the Granger Place Seminary for girls and the Fort Hills Academy for boys, each occupying old and interesting buildings. In the Granger Place School there are a few exquisite examples of Colonial furniture and several fine mantels, one of which is shown on page 193, and another, more elaborate, Frank Wallis has embodied in his book on Colonial architecture.

Perhaps the most pretentious house in the village is the Grey mansion, designed by an English architect early in the present century and built by English workmen imported for that purpose. Seen, as I saw it, just as dusk on a winter day, untenanted, in the midst of vast, desolate and gloomy grounds, it was the most forbidding human habitation conceivable, and this impression was intensified a hundred-fold by an inspection of its interior by the light of a single oil lamp as I followed the old custodian from one great echoing room to another. The finish, with the exception of a couple of bedroom mantels, is hideous. A spiral stair-

way of solid mahogany extends from the basement to an observatory on the roof, from which a fine view of the lake and the surrounding country may be obtained. My guide told me that the house contains more than sixty rooms and I could readily believe it, for it is practically four stories high, and correspondingly large in extent. Whether the place is haunted or not I do not know, but it haunts me still. There certainly never was a house offering more conveniences to ghosts of moderate means in search of suitable apartments.

At Brighton there is only one important house, the Culver homestead, now owned and occupied by Mr. Howard Smith. It was originally a tavern, the first beyond the historic Eagle Tavern at Rochester, on the direct road from Niagara Falls to Albany.

This fact accounts for some peculiarities of its arrangement and construction, the second story of the main part being principally given over to one large room—the old ballroom, which extends the entire length of the front of the house, with nine windows, facing in three directions, and two fireplaces, one on each side of the entrance. The ceiling is high and domed, and the floor sets clear of the joists so as to make it springy for the dancers and to facilitate the execution of "pigeon-wings," which were a principal feature of many of the old-time dances.

Geneva, being an old town and well to the eastward, contains many interesting Colonial buildings. The oldest is the Tillman block on Exchange Street, and architecturally considered, it is perhaps the best, following as it does the common New England type of the period in which it was built. Of quite a different character are the houses which line Main Street, the "Faubourg Saint-Germain" of the aristocratic little town. Here the Colonial style has undergone important modifications, in order better to meet unusual

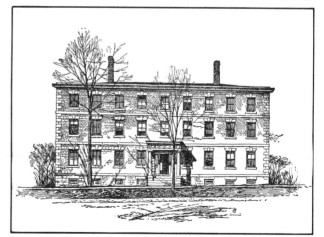

ONE OF THE HOBART COLLEGE BUILDINGS,
GENEVA, NEW YORK

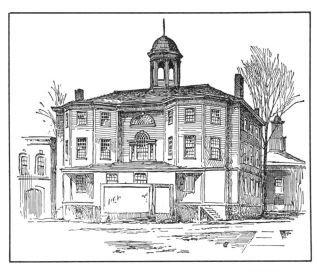

ELLICOTT HALL, BATAVIA, NEW YORK

requirements. The street skirts the summit of a high bluff overlooking Seneca Lake, and from it the view is magnificent; and the houses are accordingly provided with ample verandas, not only in the first story but in the second also. It is interesting to compare the various solutions of the difficulties in design, involved in such an arrangement. The most popular seems to have been some modification of the Classic portico with the second-story balcony let-in between the great columns, but in a few cases, two superimposed orders have been employed. The Folger House, built about 1825, may be mentioned as the best example of this class. Here by making the second-story piazza three spaces wide, above five spaces in the first, a fine pyramidal effect is obtained.

The Hobart College buildings are on Main Street at the summit of the hill. The first one was built in 1821 and the second, identical in appearance, in 1837. Though aside from the subject of Colonial architecture, I cannot refrain from an admiring mention of the beautiful English Gothic church built by Upjohn during our best Gothic period, and worthy to rank in the same high class as Grace and Trinity of New York.

Batavia, though half as many miles to the west of the Genesee as Geneva is to the east of it, was settled at about the same time. In 1800 the village was surveyed for a town, and in 1802 it was made the seat of government of the county through the efforts of one Joseph Ellicott, a surveyor and agent of the Holland Land Company, and the principal pioneer of the region immediately west of the Genesee River. The old land office and the first court house and jail are still standing. The former is unoccupied and ruinous, but is soon to be put in good condition and converted into a sort of historical museum. The latter, Ellicott Hall,

has suffered many alterations, having been used in turn as a court house, land office, a fire-insurance office, a roller-skating rink and a storehouse for second-hand furniture, which it remains. It was built in 1802 and was paid for in land, the builder receiving one acre for every day's labor. Immediately beside it, formerly stood a house to which Gen. Winfield Scott was taken, to recover from wounds received in the battles of Chippewa and Lundy's Lane, in the War of 1812; nearby was a tavern, Keye's stand, which served as officers' headquarters throughout the same war.

The early history of the region around about Batavia is mainly the history of the Holland Purchase. The land bought from the Indians by Messrs. Phelps and Gorham, through their failure to carry out their part of the agreement, reverted to its original holder, the state of Massachusetts. The part lying west of the Genesee river was then bought by Robert Morris, who sold it in 1792–1793 to an association of Dutch and American capitalists, called the Holland Land Company, he still retaining a part, under the title of the Morris Reserve. In 1797, the company employed Joseph Ellicott to survey their purchase and to open offices for the sale of the land to settlers, who shortly came flocking from the east and south. As before stated, and as the name implies, the Holland Company was composed largely of Dutchmen, and there are one or two amusing incidents recorded in the history of the purchase, which are as delightfully characteristic of the race as those narrated in Diedrich Knickerbocker's immortal history. Here is one of them: In the first apportioning of the land, for some reason not readily apparent, four members of the Willink family were given their choice of 300,000 acres in any part of the Purchase. They thereupon located it in a square found in the southeast corner, which was absolutely the most

HOUSE AT CANANDAIGUA, NEW YORK

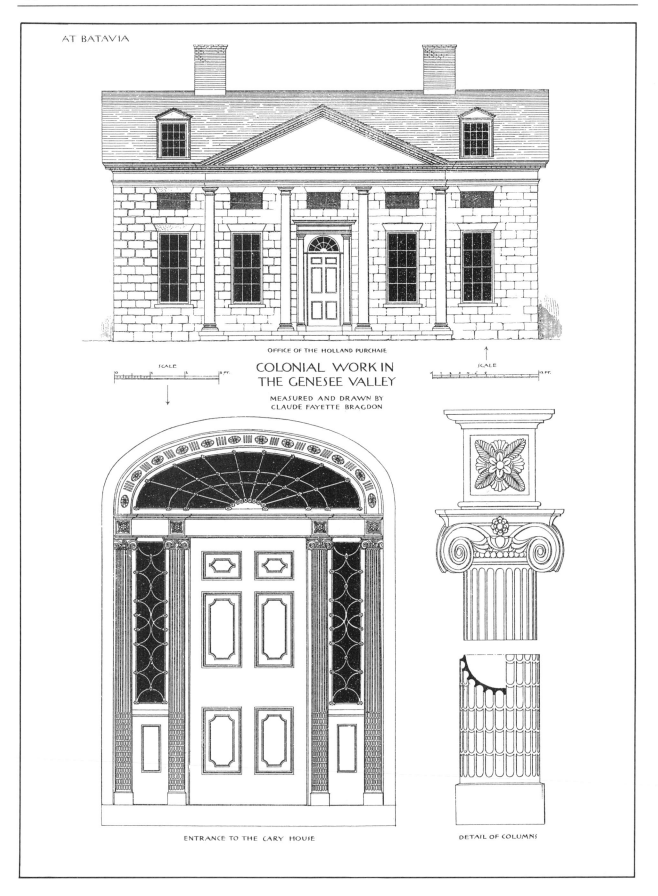

AT BATAVIA

OFFICE OF THE HOLLAND PURCHASE

SCALE

COLONIAL WORK IN
THE GENESEE VALLEY

MEASURED AND DRAWN BY
CLAUDE FAYETTE BRAGDON

SCALE

ENTRANCE TO THE CARY HOUSE

DETAIL OF COLUMNS

CARY HOUSE, BATAVIA, NEW YORK

undesirable portion of all, from an agricultural point-of-view, for no other reason than that it was *nearest to Philadelphia!*

The pioneer history of the purchase is barren of romantic interest—of "hair-breadth 'scapes, and stirring accidents by flood and field"; but there is at least one story, which, though lacking in blood-stirring and hair-raising elements, yet strangely affects the imagination and lingers long in the memory, like some minor air. It is still told to children around many firesides and is called the "Story of the Lost Boy."

In 1806, one David Tolles, a farmer living near Batavia, sent his son to watch that no cattle strayed into a newly planted field, there being no roadside fences in those days. The lad discharged his duty faithfully: when the animals appeared, he followed them out into the woods, but he never came out again. The whole countryside was aroused and search parties organized, but the mystery of his disappearance was never solved. On the second day of the search someone discovered his tracks; on the third, they found where he had slept, and the bundle of fagots which had formed his pillow; on the fourth day, they came upon a little brook where he had washed some roots—the water was yet roily with his presence—but he had fled at their approach and further search proved unavailing.

It is a sad little story, but the sequel is sadder still: From that time until the day of his death, the father of the Lost Boy became a wanderer in the vain search for his son. If a rumor reached him of a wild boy having been seen in Pennsylvania, or Ohio, or in places even more remote, he would set out on foot, only to be disappointed at his journey's end, or sent upon some equally fruitless quest. Against the plain and commonplace background of the times, the figure of this sad, mad, remorseful father looms large and black.

One cannot but picture him a very Lear of the wilderness, poor and alone, penetrating on foot the hungry fastnesses of regions little known, in search of the Lost Boy, who, if alive at all, was a boy no longer.

The village of Le Roy contains, at least, one house of more than common interest. This is the Le Roy mansion, at one time the residence of the family for which the place was named. It was built some time previous to 1812, and was originally a land office of the Holland Company, of which Herman Le Roy was an agent. In 1821 it was remodeled and enlarged, and occupied by his three sons and a daughter, Catherine Bayard Le Roy; and here, in 1828, came the great Daniel Webster, courting her. They were married the following year, she being his second wife. Shortly after the wedding a grand reception was held at the old house. Webster seems to have been fond of the place and often visited it with his wife in after years.

Traveling in the vicinity of Avon, Geneseo and Mount Morris, one can understand why the Indians gave to that region the name of the Beautiful Valley. It is like a great park. Gently sloping, wooded hills merge imperceptibly into cultivated lowlands through which the shallow river flows, sequestered in an avenue of foliage. The plain is diversified by trees and groves, and good straight roads, looking like yellow ribbons on the prim green dress of Nature, their ends concealed among the hills—lost in the tangle of her hair. Dignified old houses appear here and there, crowning the summit of some eminence, or half-hidden amid the trees of the parts with which they are engirt—their air of aloofness atoned for by the always wide-open gates, which seem to extend a perpetual invitation to the traveler. Every turn of every road reveals new vistas, new surprises. The rawness and newness, which is so constant a characteristic of most of the scenery of our agricultural districts, seem here to have been trained quite away from the landscape,

Rear
LE ROY HOUSE, LE ROY, NEW YORK

AT GENEVA

THE FOLGER HOUSE

COLONIAL WORK IN
THE GENESEE VALLEY

MEASURED AND DRAWN BY
CLAUDE FAYETTE BRAGDON

DETAIL OF ENTRANCE

DETAIL OF SECOND STORY PORCH

PIFFARD HOUSE, PIFFARD, NEW YORK

without giving place to mere smugness—the clean-shaven Philistine face of a too great prosperity. Nature is neither master nor servant, but the friend of man. Imagine, if you please, a park, from the wise hand of Olmsted, we will say, enormously enlarged and made for use as well as pleasure, and you will have formed a fairly accurate idea of this part of the Genesee country.

The curtain of history rolling up, reveals this beautiful valley the scene of a bloody drama—its denizens plunged in the most terrible kind of warfare. During the Revolution, a division of our army, under Sullivan, penetrated thus far into what was then a virgin wilderness, fighting the hostile Iroquois and setting fire to their villages. Just before the expedition reached the river, it met with its most determined resistance and sustained its severest losses, chief among which was the capture of Lieutenant Thomas Boyd and his party by the Indians. That brave officer they tortured and put to death in a manner too sickeningly horrible to be related. One prefers, rather, to dwell upon the valley's later history, which was a singularly happy and peaceful one.

Many of the early settlers came from Maryland. They were not the ordinary type of pioneer, but men of parts, possessing wealth and culture, and belonging to a class—now, unhappily, extinct—of which Washington and Jefferson are representatives. They left so great an impress on the place of their adoption that their influence is potent still, today, and this accounts in some measure for the feeling one sometimes has of a civilization older than mere dates warrant. For these first settlers did not begin anew, in pioneer fashion, but resumed, under new conditions and amid different surroundings, the lives to which they were accustomed. They built houses like the Southern houses (sometimes even to the office, at a little distance from the main building, where the business of the estate was transacted), they kept slaves, whom they had brought with them, and each family had a carriage in which its members went visiting, in true Southern fashion—sometimes driving forty miles to dine with friends.

The descendants of these people—the Wadsworths, the Fitzhughs, the Carrolls, the Piffards—own and occupy the land today and still cherish the memory and keep alive the tradition of those early days. But in the heart of New York State, time cannot be made to turn backward nor stand still. The "smart set" now invade the valley annually, and disseminate an atmosphere of *fin de siècle* worldliness, which, mingling with what survives of the colonial spirit, imparts to the social life of the place a peculiar and indefinable quality. Perhaps no other part of America is so like rural England in many ways, and it is so, not on account of any particular Anglomania on the part of any portion of its inhabitants, but because similar causes are bound to produce similar effects. As stated before, there is a class here corresponding in many particulars to the nobility of England: it is composed of hereditary landowners who lease the major portion of their land to farmers, and, living upon their estates the greater part of the year, in every way identify their interests with those of the rural population. These men lead large lives: are socially and politically important; have many friends. So, at certain seasons, when nature is at its loveliest, their houses fill with guests from abroad, and it is then that the resemblance to English country-house life becomes most marked. Fox-hunting completes the picture, and this deserves more than a passing mention.

The Genesee Valley Hunt is one of the oldest and best-known in the country, and, unlike some others, the chase is after bona fide foxes. The season opens about the end of September, and continues into the winter. The meets have the reputation of being very sportsman-like events, and not merely a new kind of "function" for the display of red coats and bob-tailed horses. The runs are increasingly long and severe, so

OLD HAMPTON, GENESEE, NEW YORK
Now destroyed

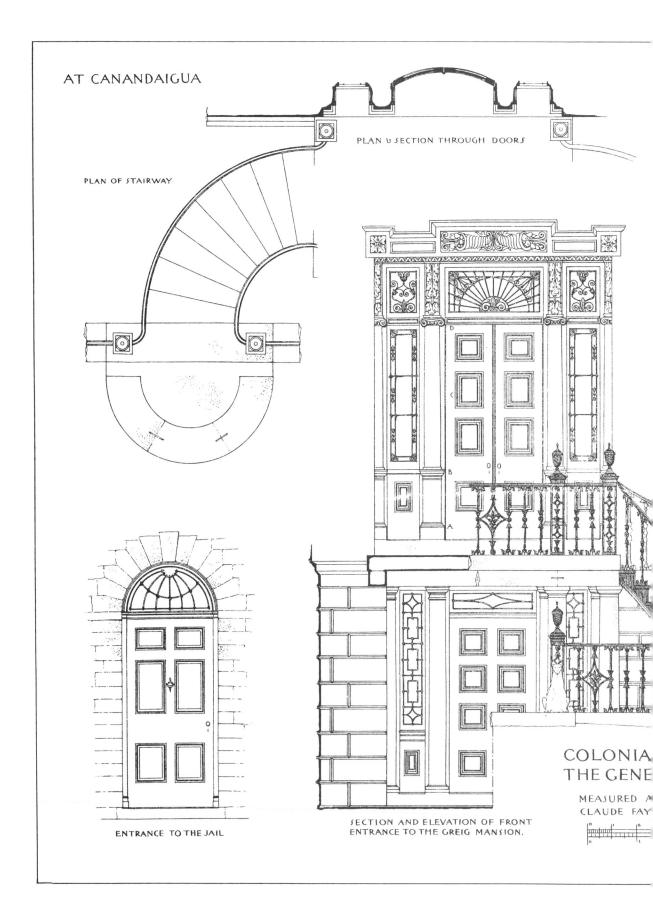

AT CANANDAIGUA

PLAN & SECTION THROUGH DOORS

PLAN OF STAIRWAY

ENTRANCE TO THE JAIL

SECTION AND ELEVATION OF FRONT
ENTRANCE TO THE GREIG MANSION.

COLONIA
THE GENE

MEASURED A
CLAUDE FAY

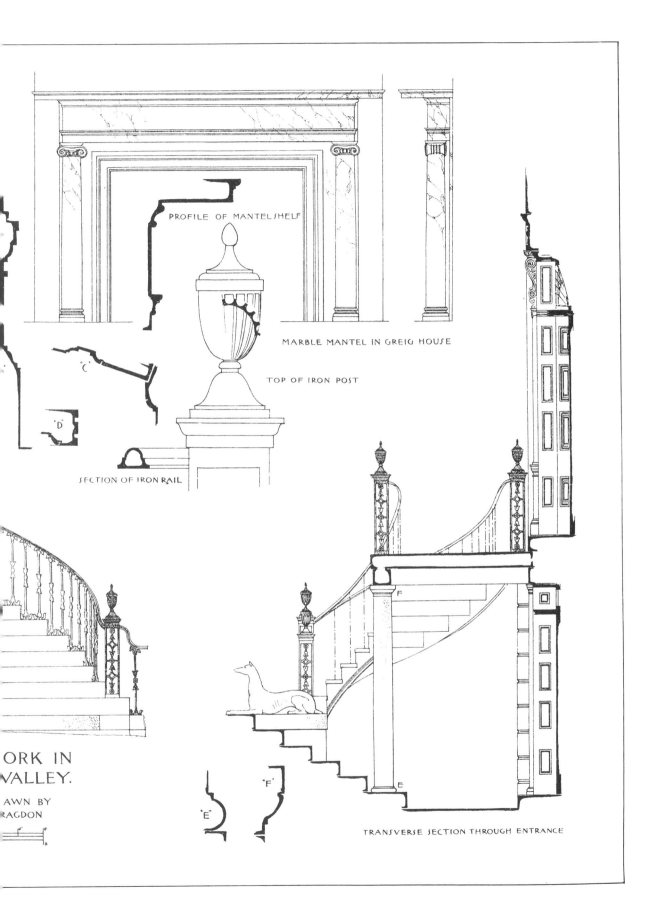

PROFILE OF MANTEL SHELF

MARBLE MANTEL IN GREIG HOUSE

TOP OF IRON POST

SECTION OF IRON RAIL

ORK IN
VALLEY.

AWN BY
RAGDON

TRANSVERSE SECTION THROUGH ENTRANCE

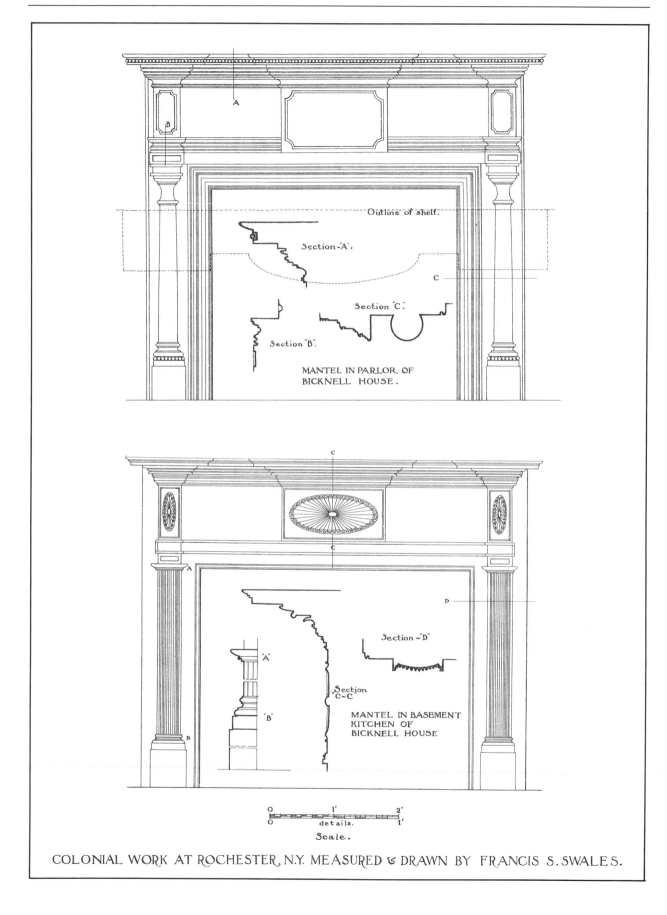

Outline of shelf.

Section "A".

C

Section "C."

Section "B".

MANTEL IN PARLOR OF
BICKNELL HOUSE.

C

C

A

D

Section "D"

"A"

Section
C~C

"B"

B

MANTEL IN BASEMENT
KITCHEN OF
BICKNELL HOUSE

O   1'   2'
O   1'
   details.
Scale.

COLONIAL WORK AT ROCHESTER, N.Y. MEASURED & DRAWN BY FRANCIS S. SWALES.

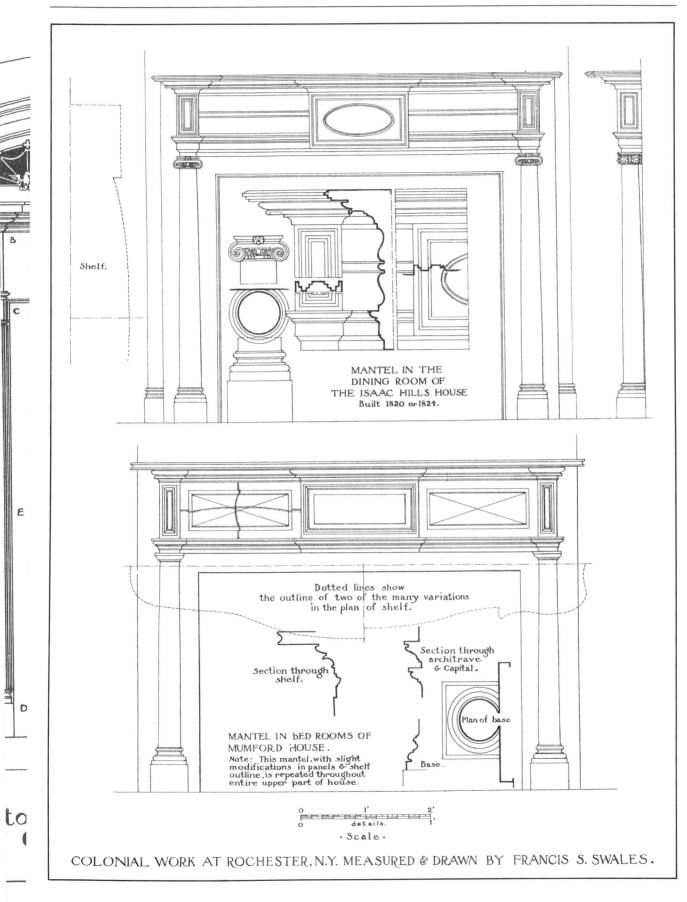

MANTEL IN THE
DINING ROOM OF
THE ISAAC HILLS HOUSE
Built 1820 or 1824.

Shelf.

Dotted lines show
the outline of two of the many variations
in the plan of shelf.

Section through
shelf.

Section through
architrave
& Capital.

Plan of base

Base.

MANTEL IN BED ROOMS OF
MUMFORD HOUSE.
Note: This mantel, with slight
modifications in panels & shelf
outline, is repeated throughout
entire upper part of house.

0   1'   2'
details.
0   1'
·Scale·

COLONIAL WORK AT ROCHESTER, N.Y. MEASURED & DRAWN BY FRANCIS S. SWALES.

FURNITURE IN POSSESSION OF
MISS A. M. PIFFARD

that no women, except the most intrepid, now participate. Anything on four legs is at liberty to follow the hounds, and the farmers of the vicinity are sometimes the most enthusiastic huntsmen. The traveling public, however little it may be interested in fox-hunting, is yet indebted to the institution for one thing, at least, and that is the Big Tree Inn at Geneseo, the existence of which would scarcely be possible were it not for the annual influx of the fox-hunting contingent, when its few rooms were warred for by Buffalonians and New Yorkers. Though supported principally by this patronage, the Big Tree Inn shines for all, and few villages can boast of a prettier, neater or cleaner little hostelry. The traditional accessories of a country hotel are all conspicuous by their absence. There is no clerk behind the desk, simply because there is no desk for him to be behind; nor is there any hand-painted, Alpine-scenery-adorned cast-iron safe to stand behind him. The tablecloths do not bear on their surface maps of the Dark Continent; there are no flies in the milk, nor dishwater in the coffee. The bedsheets are not winding-shrouds with grave-damp on them; no transoms, like the ever-open eye of Mormon, stare one into wakefulness all night — in short, it is blessedly unlike a hotel at all, but more, as the name implies, like an English tavern. Perhaps to me it has an exaggerated charm, because the Inn is an old Colonial house — the

Ayrault mansion — remodeled and enlarged.

At either end of the main street in Geneseo are the entrances to the estates of G. W. and W. A. Wadsworth. The latter occupies the homestead. Few traces of the original house remain — exteriorly, at least — it is so smothered in modern Colonial additions. The grounds surrounding both residences are charming; exhibiting the best taste in landscape gardening. A grove, in each case, screens the house from the road. A drive winds through it to the slightly elevated clearing where the house stands. The formal gardening, what there is of it, is here — affording just the necessary transition between the natural and the architectural.

The Fitzhugh House, Hampton, as it was called, was destroyed by fire ten or twelve years ago. It is said to have been one of the finest, as it was one of the oldest houses in the valley. It was built by William Fitzhugh, a Marylander, about 1815, and it had for its most distinctive feature one of those high, cool porticos which are so characteristic of Southern Colonial homes.

A drive of three miles from Geneseo, across the flats, brings one of the village of Piffard, where there is an interesting house, inhabited still by members of the family from which the place was named. Better than the house itself are the many old, rare and beautiful things which it contains; it is a veritable museum of antique furniture and china and other heirlooms of a past having its roots deep in the France and England of a former century.

In this chapter, together with the accompanying drawings, I have given a fairly representative, though far from complete, summary of the Colonial work of the Genesee country. Although meager in amount and inferior in quality, compared with that of the older and richer districts of the South and East, it has, nevertheless, seemed well worth preserving a record of it, since it possesses, in full measure, those qualities which make the style such a rebuke to almost everything that we have done (in domestic architecture, at least) since its decline. These qualities are, briefly: good sense, simplicity, elegance and refinement of detail, and, more than all else, *beauty of proportion* — the quality in which the work of the architects of today is most conspicuously lacking. If we are to have, in any sense, a *renaissance* of the Colonial style, let it be entered upon with greater knowledge, and more careful attention to the principles upon which the colonial builders worked, and by means of which they achieved such admirable results. It was principally to this end — that of furnishing additional data for the study of the style — that the present work was undertaken.

CONGREGATIONAL CHURCH, CANANDAIGUA, NEW YORK
Before alteration in 1899

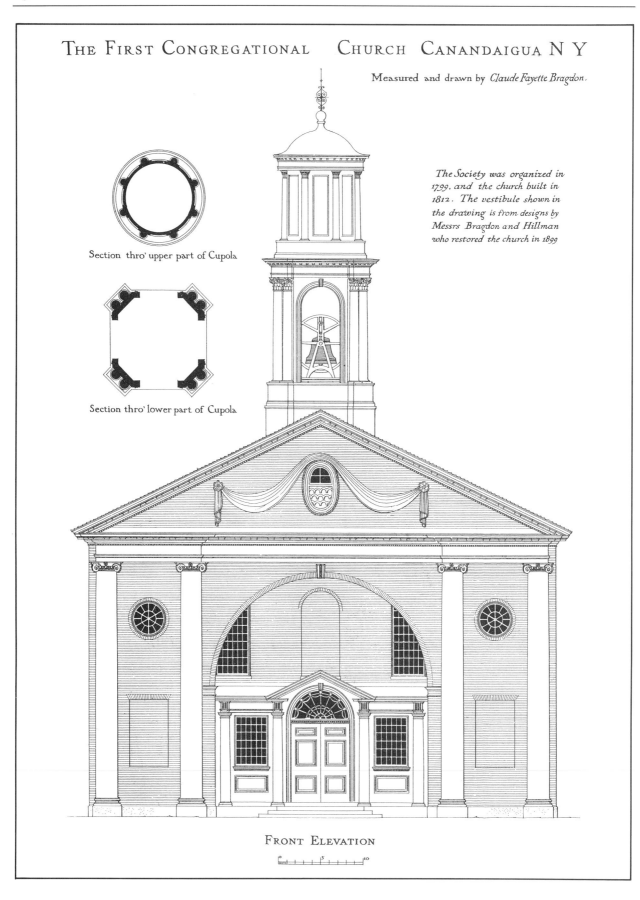

THE FIRST CONGREGATIONAL   CHURCH   CANANDAIGUA N Y

Measured and drawn by Claude Fayette Bragdon.

The Society was organized in 1799, and the church built in 1812. The vestibule shown in the drawing is from designs by Messrs Bragdon and Hillman who restored the church in 1899

Section thro' upper part of Cupola

Section thro' lower part of Cupola

FRONT ELEVATION

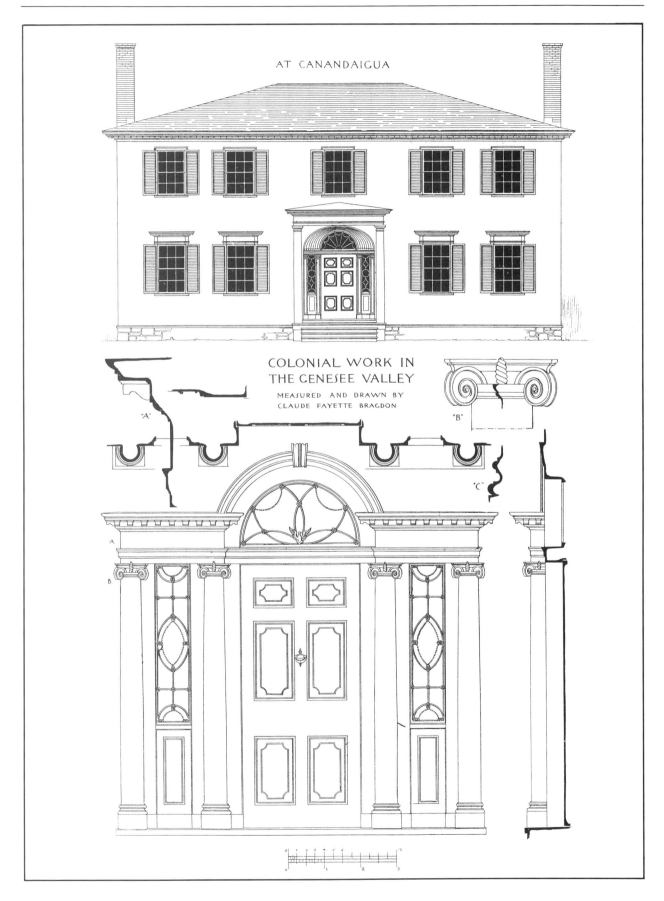

AT CANANDAIGUA

COLONIAL WORK IN
THE GENESEE VALLEY

MEASURED AND DRAWN BY
CLAUDE FAYETTE BRAGDON

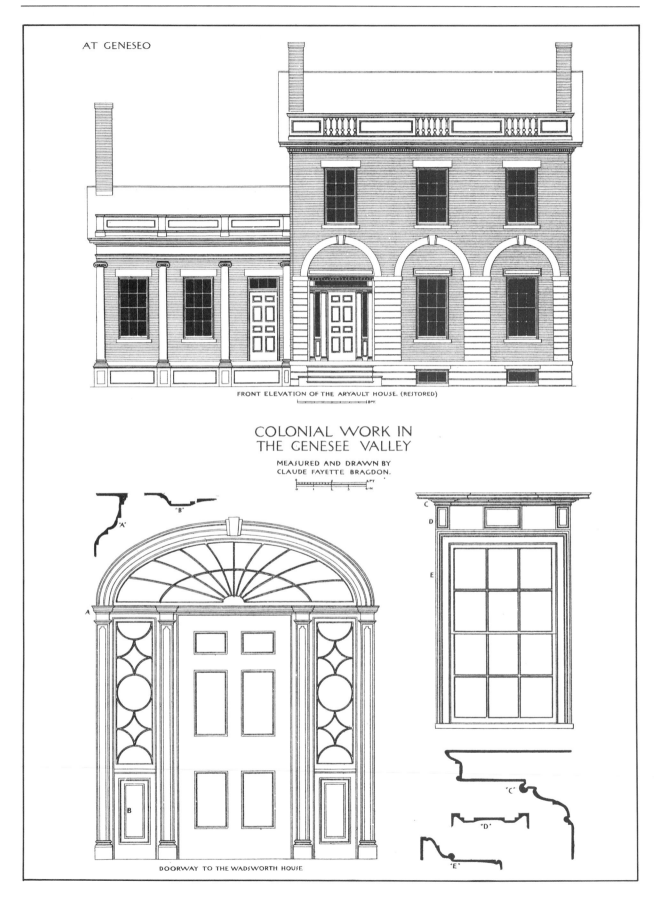

AT GENESEO

FRONT ELEVATION OF THE ARYAULT HOUSE. (RESTORED)

COLONIAL WORK IN
THE GENESEE VALLEY

MEASURED AND DRAWN BY
CLAUDE FAYETTE BRAGDON.

DOORWAY TO THE WADSWORTH HOUSE

AT CANANDAIGUA

THE ONTARIO COUNTY JAIL   BUILT IN 1815, BY JOHN DOANE, ARCHT.

INLAID BRASS ORNAMENT

BEDROOM MANTEL IN THE
GRANGER PLACE SCHOOL.

COLONIAL WORK IN
THE GENESEE VALLEY
MEASURED AND DRAWN BY
CLAUDE FAYETTE BRAGDON

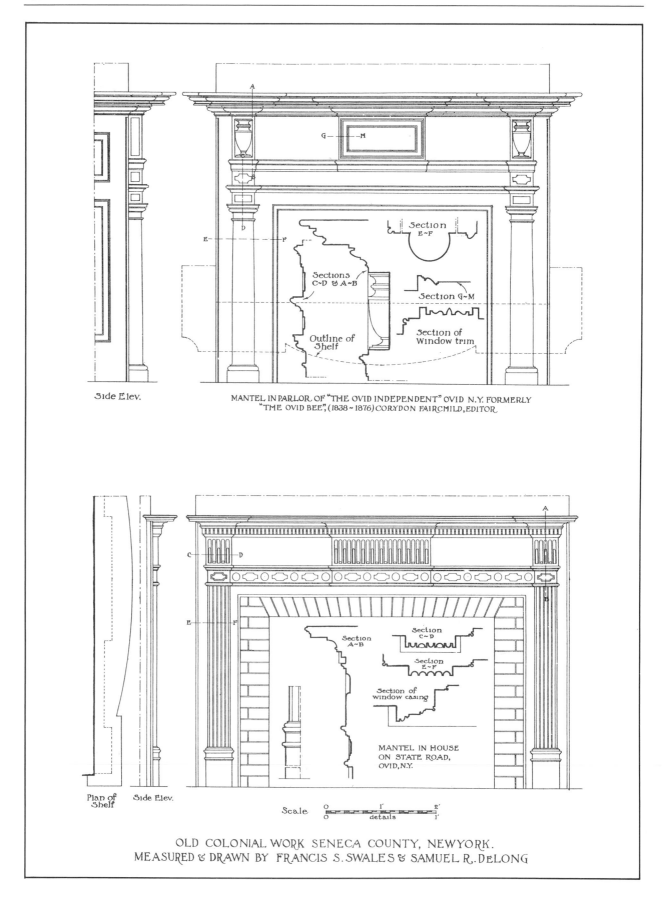

Side Elev.

MANTEL IN PARLOR OF "THE OVID INDEPENDENT" OVID N.Y. FORMERLY
"THE OVID BEE", (1838~1876) CORYDON FAIRCHILD, EDITOR

Section E~F

Sections C~D & A~B

Section G~M

Outline of Shelf

Section of Window trim

Section A~B

Section C~D

Section E~F

Section of window casing

MANTEL IN HOUSE ON STATE ROAD, OVID, N.Y.

Plan of Shelf   Side Elev.

Scale   details

OLD COLONIAL WORK SENECA COUNTY, NEW YORK.
MEASURED & DRAWN BY FRANCIS S. SWALES & SAMUEL R. DeLONG

AT GENESEO

WRÓT IRON GRILLE IN POST OFFICE.

COLONIAL WORK IN
THE GENESEE VALLEY

MEASURED AND DRAWN BY
CLAUDE FAYETTE BRAGDON

FRONT ENTRANCE TO THE COURT-HOUSE

SECTION.

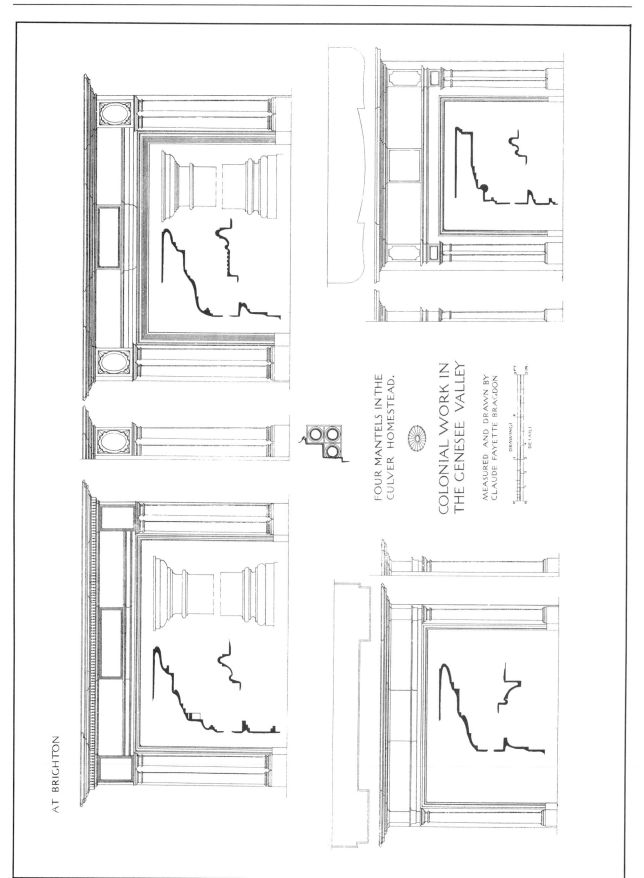

AT BRIGHTON

FOUR MANTELS IN THE
CULVER HOMESTEAD.

COLONIAL WORK IN
THE GENESEE VALLEY

MEASURED AND DRAWN BY
CLAUDE FAYETTE BRAGDON

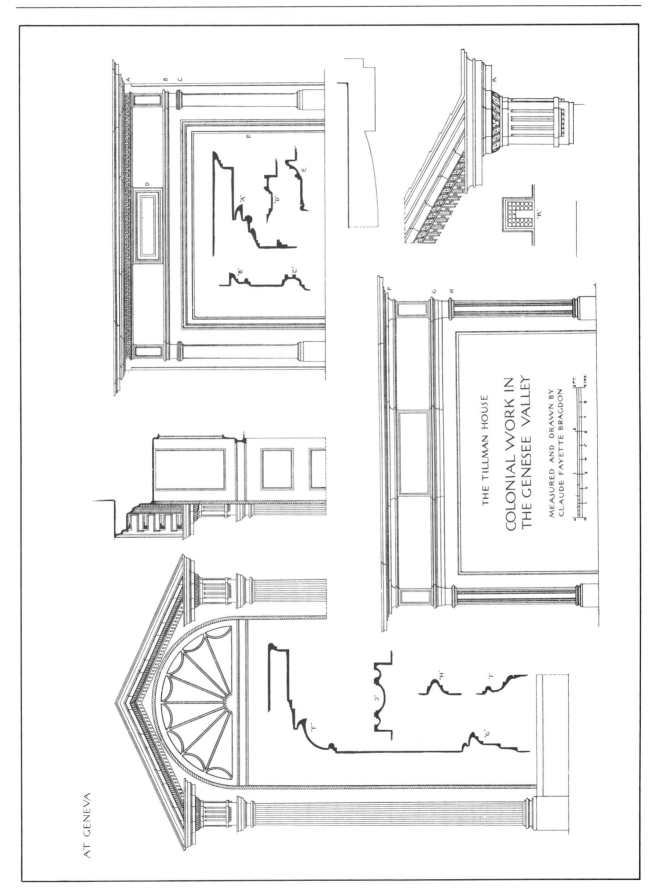

AT GENEVA

THE TILLMAN HOUSE

COLONIAL WORK IN
THE GENESEE VALLEY

MEASURED AND DRAWN BY
CLAUDE FAYETTE BRAGDON

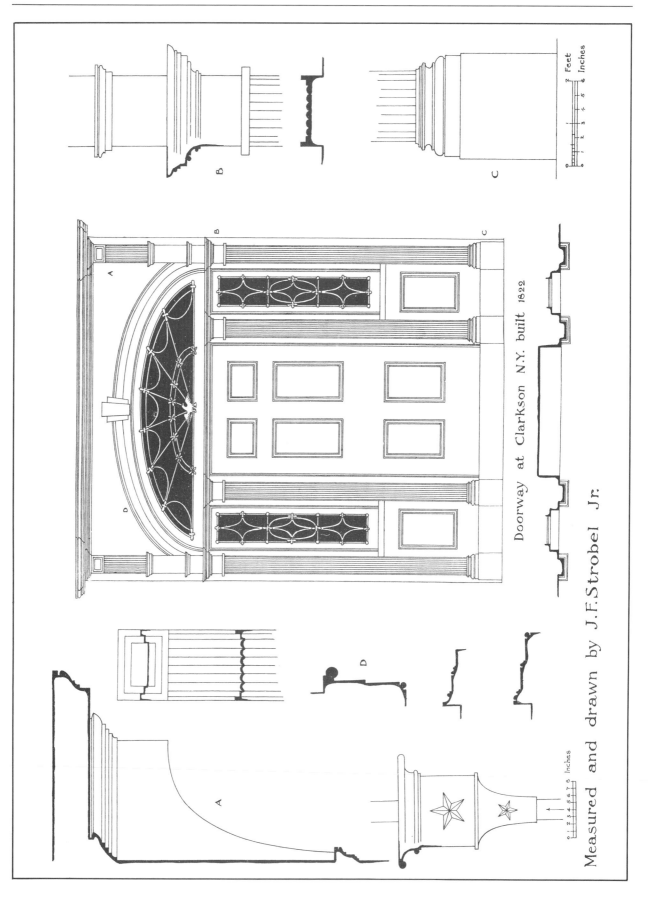

Doorway at Clarkson N.Y. built 1822

Measured and drawn by J.F.Strobel Jr.

The Mappa House
Trenton, New York

Text by
W. S. Wicks
Originally published in 1900 as
Volume II of The Georgian Period

Front Door
MAPPA HOUSE — 1809–1812 — TRENTON, NEW YORK

THE MAPPA HOUSE, TRENTON, NEW YORK

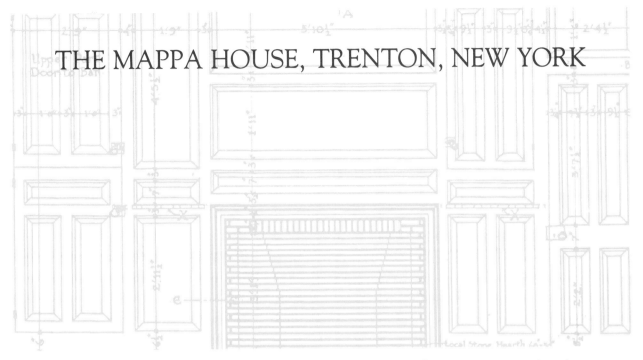

THE deadly hostility between the Patriots and the Tories, and the raids of the Indians, put a stop to all improvements in the Mohawk Valley and adjoining country until about the year 1775.

In 1793, Garrett Boone, the first agent of the Holland Land Company in this vicinity, reached the fording place of the Mohawk at Fort Schuyler (now Utica), near the place where the present Deerfield turnpike crosses the river, on his way to survey, prior to purchasing, a tract of land known as Services' Patent. From Fort Schuyler the land extended in a northerly direction. Through the virgin forest Boone blazed the trees for the line of a future road.

Reaching a "sheltered valley where two creeks come together," he pitched his tent and determined that the land about the junction of the creeks should be the site of a future village. Boone named the village site Olden Barneveld, after John of Barneveld, a famous Netherlands statesman. It is a pity that the name was changed in 1833 to its present name, Trenton. Olden Barneveld was incorporated April 19, 1819, reincorporated as Trenton, April 26, 1833. (See *New York Civil List;* 1868, page 571).

Col. Adam G. Mappa soon followed Boone to Olden Barneveld as second agent for the Holland Land Company. With him came Judge Adrian Van der Kemp, a man of brilliant education. He translated for Governor De Witt Clinton the old Dutch records belonging to the New Amsterdam government prior to English possession and government. Colonel Mappa and Judge Van der Kemp were close friends. They both built houses in the village, each now standing on opposite sides of the same street. In these houses were entertained Van Buren, De Witt Clinton, Horatio Seymour and many other notables.

The Mappa House (now owned by Mr. William S. Wicks), the subject of these illustrations, was begun in 1809, and finished at the close of the War of 1812. It was intended to be much more sumptuous, but the rise in the cost of material and labor in consequence of the war made it necessary to curtail in many ways. The Holland Land Company had allowed Colonel Mappa $15,000 for the work, but before the house was completed, he had used up this sum and much more with it.

The house stands in the center of the village square, formerly in the center of a much larger property, early reduced in size by the sale of building lots, the Madam Decastro house lot and the Unitarian Church lot being taken from the south side, the village stores and blacksmith shop lots from the northwest. The property on the northeast, on which the John Billings House stood, is now used as a village park. The deeds of conveyance of these old properties are in many ways curious; the deed of one property reads, "beginning at the corner of an asparagus bed." We presume that the fondness of the Dutch for asparagus made them feel that such a bed should last forever.

The Mappa House is 52 feet wide and 66 feet deep. The rooms in the first as well as the second story are 12 feet in height. The exterior and basement walls are of Trenton limestone, the foundations from grade to water-table being laid of five equal courses. These courses, as well as the square-faced water-table, stone

MAPPA HOUSE — 1809–1812 — TRENTON, NEW YORK

MAPPA HOUSE — 1809–1812 — TRENTON, NEW YORK

Dining Room Mantel

MAPPA HOUSE — 1809–1812 — TRENTON, NEW YORK

Library Mantel
MAPPA HOUSE — 1809–1812 — TRENTON, NEW YORK

MAPPA HOUSE
TRENTON N.Y.
Now owned by W. S. Wicks Esq.

SITTING ROOM MANTEL

Shelf Profile

Scale
12

1 2 3 4 5 6

Details

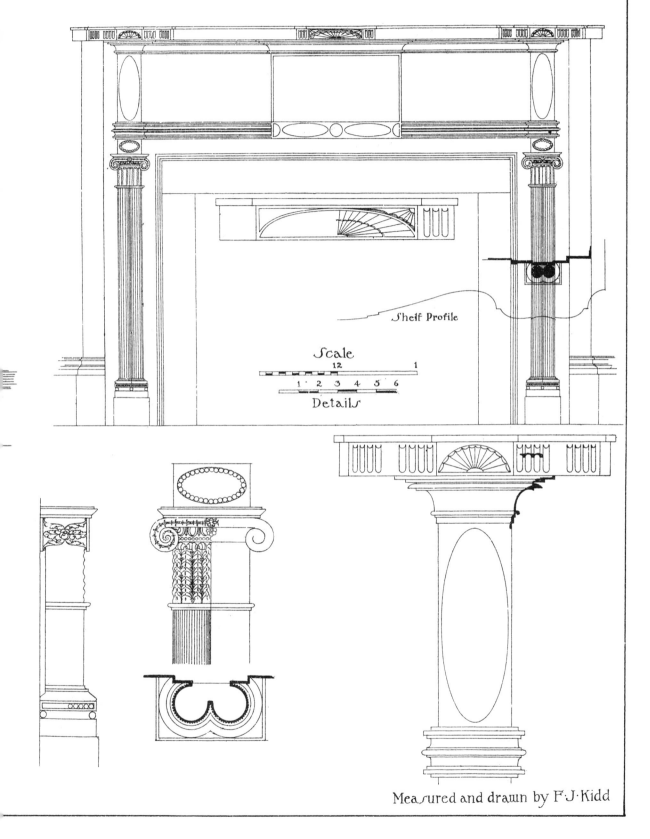

Shelf Profile

Scale

Details

Measured and drawn by F·J·Kidd

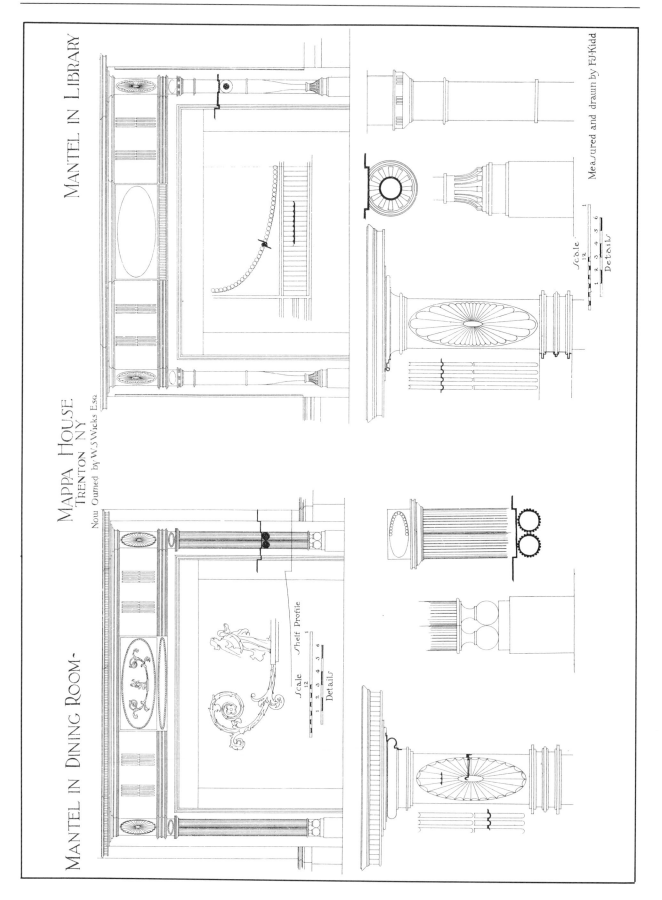

MANTEL IN LIBRARY

MAPPA HOUSE
TRENTON NY
Now Owned by W.S.Wicks Esq

MANTEL IN DINING ROOM-

Measured and drawn by F.J.Kidd

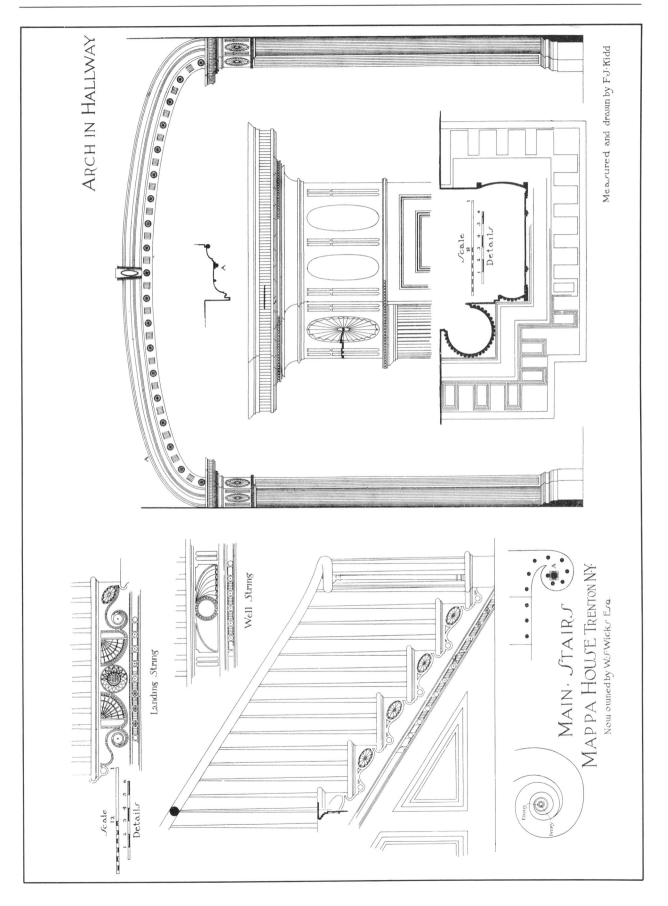

ARCH IN HALLWAY

Measured and drawn by F·J·Kidd

Scale
Details

MAIN · STAIRS
MAPPA HOUSE TRENTON N.Y.
Now owned by W·F·Wicks Esq.

Landing String

Well String

Scale
Details

Parlor Door
MAPPA HOUSE—1809–1812—TRENTON,
NEW YORK

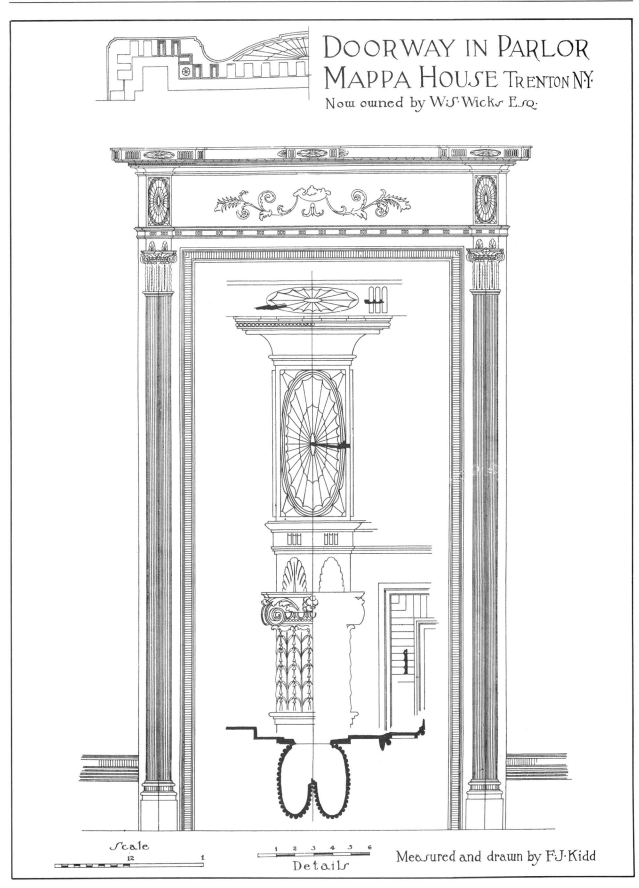

DOORWAY IN PARLOR
MAPPA HOUSE TRENTON N·Y·
Now owned by W·S· Wicks E·sq·

Scale
12 1

1 2 3 4 5 6
Details

Measured and drawn by F·J·Kidd

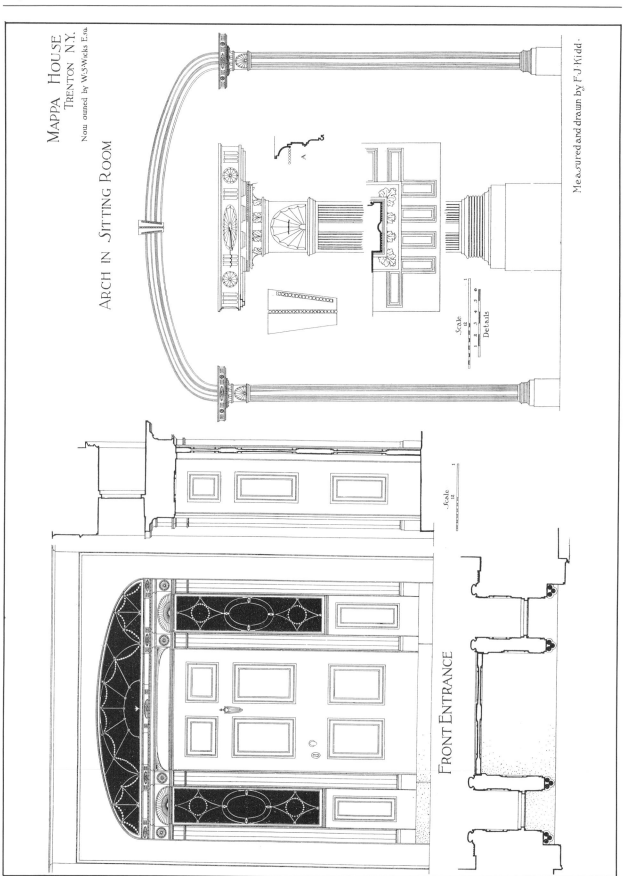

MAPPA HOUSE
TRENTON N.Y.
Now owned by W·S·Wicks Esq.

ARCH IN SITTING ROOM

Measured and drawn by F·J·Kidd.

Scale
12
Details

Scale
12

FRONT ENTRANCE

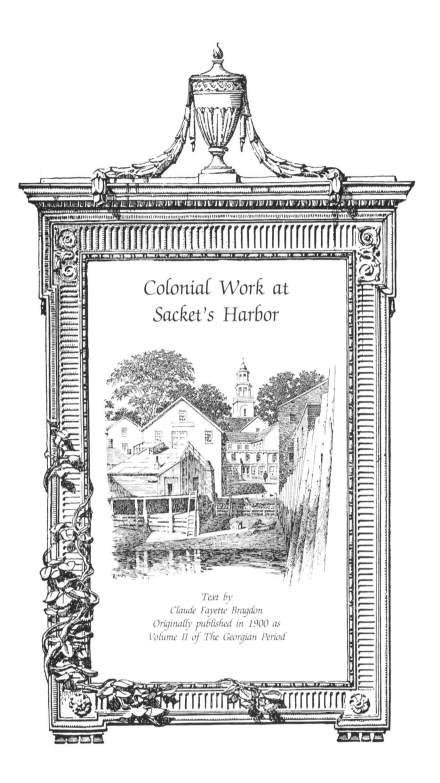

Colonial Work at Sacket's Harbor

Text by
Claude Fayette Bragdon
Originally published in 1900 as
Volume II of The Georgian Period

ARCHWAY IN THE CAMP MANSION AT SACKET'S HARBOR, N.Y.

Measured and drawn by *Claude Fayette Bragdon*

Scale of Elevation   3 ft

Scale of Details   3 in

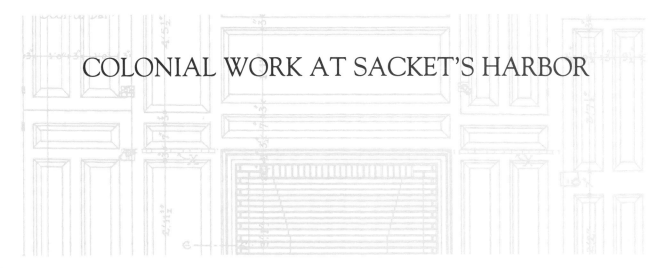

COLONIAL WORK AT SACKET'S HARBOR

SACKET'S Harbor is chiefly notable as an important military station on our northern frontier. It occupies a high, wind-swept bluff overlooking Lake Ontario. A little bay sweeps in and forms a natural harbor, which is further protected by a long, low breakwater, on which grows a line of stunted willows, leaning all one way—mute evidences of the force and direction of the prevailing winds. On one side of the bay are the barracks—a group of stone buildings, old and low, flanking three sides of a well-kept parade-ground, the fourth being open to the water's edge, where a few shapeless mounds of earth mark the location of an old pioneer fort. Inland, behind the barracks, is a cemetery, where lie buried upwards of fifteen hundred nameless soldiers, killed in battles of the War of 1812. The first gun of that war was fired from the promontory on the other side of the bay. The battlefield is now an unkempt pasture in which the village street almost loses itself and then recovers to take a final plunge over the rocks into the lake.

This first battle seems not to have been a great affair, but in the accounts of it one hears—in the hotel or barber shop, from the mouths of oldest inhabitants—there are pleasing suggestions of British swagger and of Yankee grit and resource. Five men-of-war (so goes the story), carrying some eighty guns and fully manned, suddenly appeared before the frightened inhabitants of the little town, who had for their defense only the little brig *Oneida* of seventeen guns, under Lieutenant Woolsey—but it was David and Goliath over again, as the event proved. Prevented from escape by water, Woolsey and his sailing-master landed with a company of marines and manned a thirty-two-pounder on the bluff. They had no shot large enough for the gun, but, equal to the emergency, the twenty-four-pound balls were wrapped to size with cuttings from carpets and, when these were gone, the flannel petticoats of the women. With these unique projec-

tiles the British fleet was disabled, and actually driven from the waters.

In the war which followed, Sacket's Harbor was a center of activity. Here the army was organized and the navy constructed. It was from this point that Gen. Zebulon Pike—he who gave Pike's Peak its name—started on that secret and perilous expedition in which he lost his life, and his body now lies in the old burying-ground behind the barracks. Nor is Pike's the only illustrious name associated with the place. Gen. Jacob Brown made it his headquarters while he commanded the forces on the Canadian frontier. Here lived Dr. Samuel Guthrie, one of the discoverers of chloroform and the inventor of the percussion compound for fire-arms which superseded flints. Grant was stationed here for a short period after his Mexican campaign, and there is a barrack-room story about a bet he made and won—that he could walk around the long public square at Watertown before another man could eat an army cracker, without water.

In former times the little bay was filled with shipping and Sacket's was a place of commercial as well as military importance, as the ruined old stone mills and an abandoned railroad even now testify. Those palmy days are now long past, and as there has been no subsequent revival of prosperity, the town remains today very much as it was then—happily free from the blighting and vulgarizing influence of the "great American hustler." The military atmosphere is all that remains to remind one of its departed greatness, but this is all pervasive. Every vista contains a blue uniform; dogs are numerous and barbers prosperous; the children have a soldierly bearing and one even fancies that the little brick and wooden stores elbow one another along the sidewalk of the principal street like a company of raw recruits on parade.

There is society of a certain sort, as is inevitable where idle men and women of the commanding class

MADISON BARRACKS, SACKET'S HARBOR, NEW YORK

are brought together. It is made up of officers and their wives and daughters and a few remaining representatives of the old families still living in the houses built by their grandfathers—but these, too, are military, and the number of retired colonels one may meet of an afternoon brings to mind Gilbert's witty line,

"When everybody's somebody, nobody's anybody."

With the summer weather people come here from the great world outside, infusing a new spirit into the officer's balls and other garrison festivities. Then there is tennis on the parade-ground and yachting on the bay; teas and card parties are given in the great old houses, the dingy portraits on whose walls looked down perhaps on not so very different scenes in times long gone.

It is of these houses—some of them—I wish particularly to speak. Aside from their historical associations, they are intrinsically excellent in architecture. This, though lacking much of the richness and elaboration of some of the Eastern and Southern Colonial work, is characterized by great elegance of proportion and refinement of detail. This lack of excessive ornamentation, though probably dictated by motives of economy, is, on the whole, fortunate, for architecture often gains rather than loses by such enforced simplicity, just as "an honest tale speeds best, being plainly told."

Although there is much good and interesting work beside, there are only three houses in any way deserving the title of "mansion," and to the task of preserving some sort of a record of them, the present writer devoted a few days of a short vacation spent in the vicinity in the early nineties. This work, if valuable, was timely, as one of the three was already falling to pieces through age and neglect, and another had recently undergone extensive alterations in order to more nearly fulfill the requirements of modern life.

The Sacket House was built in 1803 by August Sacket, from whom the town received its name. It is square in plan, with a long wing to the rear. The second story is lighted entirely by dormers, and the exterior is thereby rendered very effective by reason of the ample space above the tops of the first-story windows. The low, broad façade, with its well-proportioned columns and pediment, seen from the main street above the large, old-fashioned garden, produces that rarest of earthly things—a genuine architectural emotion. The interior is less interesting. There is very little woodwork, and that little is quite lacking in refinement. This house served as a hospital during the War of 1812, and blood stains may yet be seen on the upstairs floors—so it is said.

On the Battlefield
SACKET'S HARBOR, NEW YORK

SACKET HOUSE, SACKET'S HARBOR, NEW YORK

The Woolsey mansion, now owned and occupied by Col. Walter B. Camp, was built in 1816 by Commodore Woolsey. The knocker on the front door bears, quite appropriately, the shape of an American eagle, and behind the door there is a row of big wooden pegs, where, we are told, the Commodore used always to hang his hat on entering. In plan, the house is a departure from the usual type, the hall being at the side of the main part, instead of in the center; there are two rooms adjoining, and the wings contain two more, with pantries and the like. As originally built, there were but two bedrooms on the second floor, the servants' sleeping-rooms being located in the basement.

The old Commodore's love of formality and symmetry is apparent in the laying out of the grounds and outbuildings. The house sets far back from the road, and is approached through a central gateway flanked on each side by smaller ones, for pedestrians. The drive is lined with trees and shrubbery, and the white central pavilion of the house, with its slenderly pillared portico, is thus seen at the end of a green vista.

Nowhere is anything allowed to interfere with symmetry, the rear being as perfect in this respect as the front. A few rods behind the house a fence divides the lawn from the garden, and this is made another opportunity for a piece of formal grouping, charming in its effect. On one side is the well-house and on the other the smokehouse, both alike, of stone, with segment-shaped roofs: between the two, surmounting a low wall, is a white fence of delicate design, with frequent posts. In the center this fence forms a semicircle, in the middle of which is the garden gate, flanked by two large posts: the path leads to a summerhouse, which occupies the center of the garden.

Some of the old furniture still remains in the house, notably a number of tables of very graceful outline, beautifully inlaid.

The Camp mansion, or "The Brick," as it is called, was built in 1816 by Col. Elisha Camp, an officer of artillery in the War of 1812. It is now tenanted, from June till October, by the family of his granddaughter, Mrs. Col. Mason. It is a most substantial structure, built of brick brought from England for the purpose. The cellar-bottom is formed by the living rock. The plan is of the common Colonial type: there is a wide hall in the center, with two rooms on each side and a one-story addition to the rear overlooking the garden, which contains what used to be the children's rooms

WOOLSEY HOUSE, SACKET'S
HARBOR, NEW YORK

that even now, though used constantly, it shows few signs of wear.

The original "scenic" paper is on the walls; on either side of the fireplace are graceful wall-tables, semi-elliptical in shape, and between the windows there is an old upright piano in mahogany and gold, the first ever brought into the country, and considered a grand and wonderful affair when it was new. Some of the up-stairs bedrooms are extremely bright and pretty. There are old-fashioned, high-post bedsteads, with canopies above, and dressing tables of quaint and now obsolete patterns. Woodwork and draperies are all pure white, the door panels alone being tinted a light blue, with good effect. There is a great attic over the entire house, lighted at the ends by enormous semicircular windows. Here are stored old beds, clocks and spinning wheels, and trunks and chests and boxes, among

Front Entrance
CAMP MANSION, SACKET'S
HARBOR, NEW YORK

·and nursery. The main hall is divided into vestibule, reception hall and stair hall by means of arches with elliptical fanlight transoms above. These arches contain mahogany doors in four folds, the two central ones being used on ordinary occasions; while in the hot days of summer, or when the house is thrown open for purposes of entertainment, all are folded back out of the way against the wall, making of the hall one large apartment. This seems a good solution of a much-vexed problem in house-planning: to obtain necessary divisions between the parts of the hall possessing different functions, without impairing its spaciousness or embarrassing the movements of a crowd of guests.

Some of the rooms remain just as they were when the house was built. The same carpet has been on the parlor floor for over seventy years; it was woven in England to fit the room, and is of such good material

MABEE HOUSE, SCHENECTADY, NEW YORK

which one might delightedly rummage away the hours of the longest of rainy Sundays — if the opportunity offered.

These few random notes may add interest to the accompanying sketches and measured drawings. Young architects and draughtsmen throughout the country are apt to complain of the complete lack of sources of architectural inspiration in their environment, while, perhaps, at their very doors are unheeded examples of a refined and even scholarly treatment of wood — the very material in which nine-tenths of their designing must needs be done. If such would hunt up old houses in their vicinity, and by measurements and sketches convey to paper what they find valuable therein, they would not only be individually profited thereby, but would also be assisting to preserve a lasting record of the now fast-diminishing remnants of the only good and characteristic architecture this country has yet succeeded in producing.

MABEE HOUSE, SCHENECTADY, NEW YORK

This house, which we believe is still standing, was built, in 1706, for use in the first place as a farmstead, and in the second, as a fort to which the owner and his neighbors could retire in time of need. The building is 22′ x 48′, with walls about three feet thick, of rough mountain stone, laid at the time of building in clay. At a later day the joints have been raked and pointed with lime mortar. The lower story is about eight feet in the clear, the ceiling beams, 12″ x 18″, acting as tie-beams pinning the feet of the rafters together and forming with them an equilateral truss. — WARE

OLD HOUSE AT MADISON, NEW JERSEY

Although we know nothing about this building, neither its history, nor its age, it is, nevertheless, typical of a class of houses which are found in considerable numbers in northern New Jersey. It is here shown because it seems to furnish a real connecting link between the type-plan of the southern builders and that of their northern fellows. The treatment of the roof of the central building distinctly shows its descent from the buildings of the Dutch colonist, while the wings upon either side as distinctly recall the wing galleries, with which the southern designer habitually connected his main house with the end pavilions, often devoted on the one side to bachelor apartments and on the other to the kitchen or house-servants. — WARE

OLD HOUSE AT MADISON, NEW JERSEY

FRONT ELEVATION of the SACKET HOUSE.

DOOR LATCH

TRANSOM LIGHT.

LOCK PLATE

4'-7"

DINING ROOM MANTEL

LEG

Brass shoe

BRASS

MEASURED AND DRAWN BY
CLAUDE FAYETTE BRAGDON

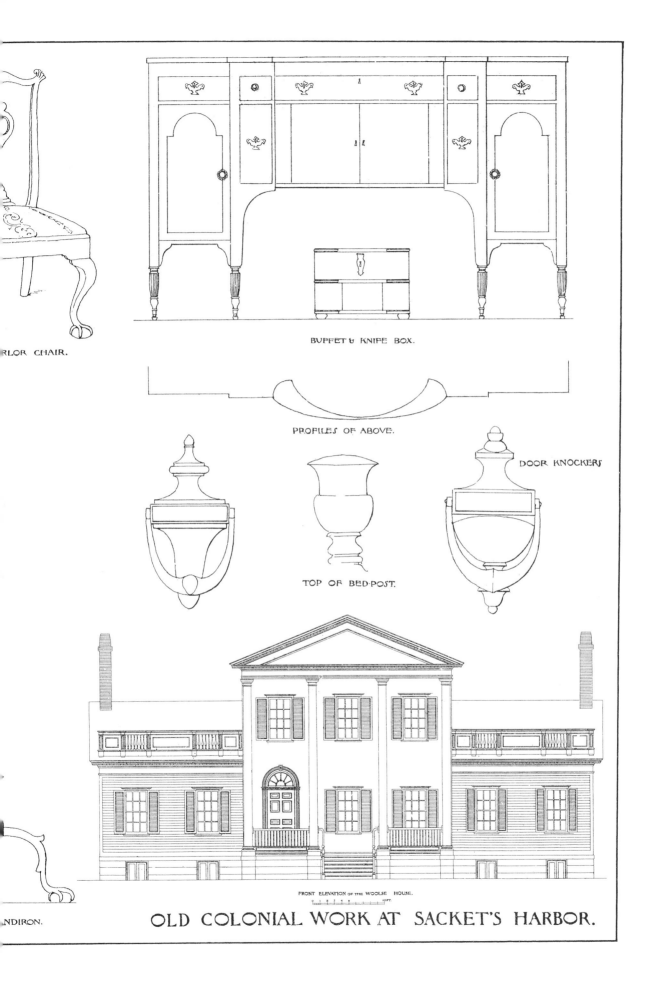

RLOR CHAIR.

BUFFET & KNIFE BOX.

PROFILES OF ABOVE.

DOOR KNOCKERS

TOP OF BED-POST.

FRONT ELEVATION OF THE WOOLSE HOUSE.

NDIRON.

OLD COLONIAL WORK AT SACKET'S HARBOR.

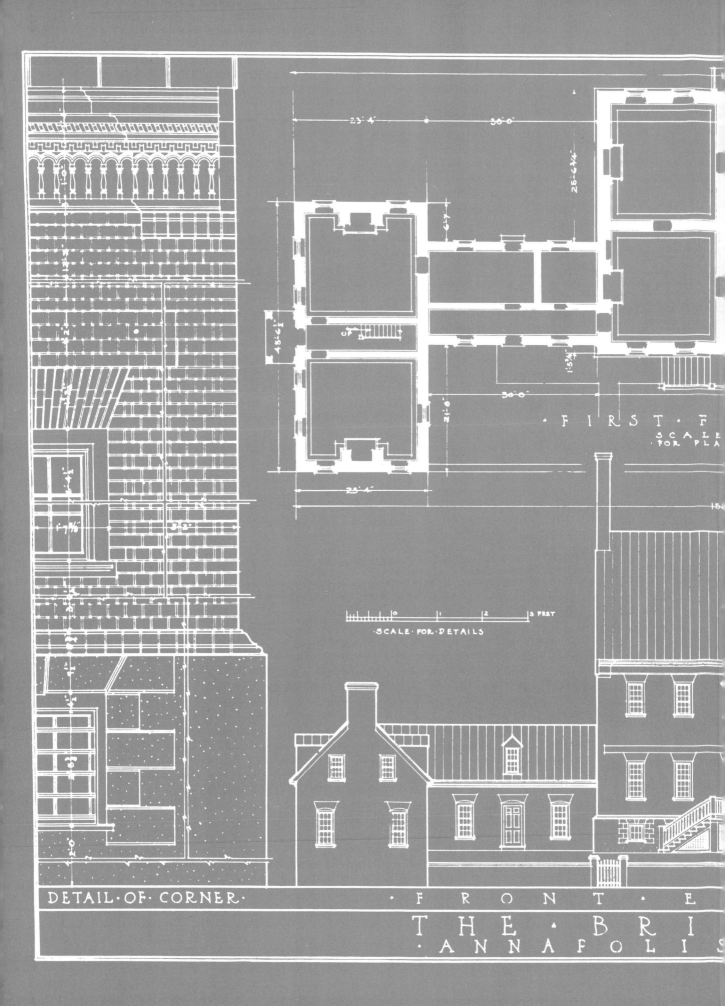

DETAIL·OF·CORNER·   · F R O N T · E

· T H E · B R I

· A N N A P O L I S

·SCALE·FOR·DETAILS·

· F I R S T · F

·FIRST·F

·SCALE

·FOR·PLA